Transforming an Idea Into a Business with Design Thinking

The Structured Approach from Silicon Valley for Entrepreneurs and Leaders

Transforming an Idea Into a Business with Design Thinking

The Structured Approach from Silicon Valley for Entrepreneurs and Leaders

By

Mashhood Alam

A PRODUCTIVITY PRESS BOOK

First edition published in 2019
by Routledge/Productivity Press
711 Third Avenue, New York, NY 10017, USA
2 Park Square, Milton Park, Abingdon, Oxon OX14 4RN, UK

© 2019 by Mashhood Alam
Routledge/Productivity Press is an imprint of Taylor & Francis Group, an Informa business

No claim to original U.S. Government works

Printed on acid-free paper

International Standard Book Number-13: 978-1-138-57760-2 (Hardback)
International Standard Book Number-13: 978-1-138-57759-6 (Paperback)
International Standard Book Number-13: 978-1-351-26656-7 (eBook)

Visit the Taylor & Francis website at
http://www.taylorandfrancis.com

This book is dedicated to:

Abba, my grandfather, whose love for knowledge is captured aptly in the title of his book as "thirst of a sieve";

my parents, especially Ammi, my mother, whose unconditional love is the foundation of my being

Tabassum, my wife and best friend, whose selfless support made this book possible;

and Wasi, Aleena and Inayah, my children, whose smiles brighten my life.

Contents

Foreword

Entrepreneurs hate reading books. They want to do things. And fast. I know. I am an entrepreneur. And that is exactly why most start-ups fail. Of course, there are many factors that contribute to a start-up's demise, but chief among them is when leaders jump to a solution without fully understanding and appreciating the problem.

This is exactly why this book is needed – it is designed to provide a checklist and a method for understanding (1) what users and customers want, and (2) how to more fully comprehend the unmet need before launching a solution. Design Thinking has been around for a long time but only recently has been accepted as an essential method for conceiving products and solutions while empathizing with the user.

I am so glad to see that Mashhood, whom I have known for several years in Silicon Valley, was able to view the essence of design thinking as applicable to any entrepreneur. Most books on entrepreneurship focus on the mechanics of getting funding or the journey of an entrepreneur. Starting with the user of the solution as the focal point is exactly how entrepreneurs should be thinking. This is the book to lead us in that direction.

With precise techniques and methods, an entrepreneur can start to empathize with the user. I am confident that if entrepreneurs read this book and follow the cogent advice and method outlined by the author, we will see far more start-up success stories – both in terms of finding the perfect product-market fit and scale, and in terms of financial returns.

This book is a much-needed and relevant work – one of significant importance in today's rapidly changing world. Regular jobs are disappearing, and more and more people will be taking on entrepreneurial endeavors to succeed.

Even though technology plays a dominant role in emerging business models (and will continue to do so), the focus on human centricity has never been more pronounced. Design Thinking puts the importance of human centricity at the core of problem solving. Focusing on the user's current journey in order to identify opportunities and craft a vision for future experiences is an extremely valuable way of approaching a new venture. Today, user experience is everything.

There are many books out there about Design Thinking, agile development, and business models. But this book brings the three concepts together in an easy-to-use, structured framework that adds tremendous value to the entrepreneurial ecosystem.

The step-by-step approach devised by Mashhood will be extremely useful for budding entrepreneurs and product managers alike.

This book is unique in its bringing a holistic framework together. Many entrepreneurship books focus on specific angles of a new venture – funding, financial projections, marketing, business regulations, registration, and so on. Those are all very valuable, but they address only the "How" of a new venture. This book will help uncover the "Why."

Mashhood's business model framework is grounded in the value proposition for the key stakeholders, and it will enable entrepreneurs to have honest conversations about what makes their idea tick. This framework very succinctly places value at the center and helps entrepreneurial teams figure out how to not just create and deliver the value but also how to capture and fund the value.

In addition, the framework also brings forth the importance of looking beyond an entrepreneur's idea into the key trends impacting his or her business model today and tomorrow.

This book also walks the reader through each step and how to think about particular aspects of the business.

Mashhood's unique approach pushes the entrepreneurial team into explicitly thinking about assumptions they are making in all aspects of the venture and into documenting them so they do not drop the ball as the craziness of the new venture creation envelops their lives. This is one of the most important and most easily forgotten aspects of many new ventures. Having an account of these assumptions will help entrepreneurs in understanding and mitigating risks.

Raising money for start-ups is what I have done all my life. Having raised close to $100 million for seven start-ups (and having advised many more), I can tell you that it all comes down to your ability to tell a compelling story.

This is the book that allows you to see how the product or service you want to create will transform the lives of your users and helps you tell that story in the most effective way possible.

Naeem Zafar
University of California, Berkeley
Founder and CEO of TeleSense
Silicon Valley, California

Naeem Zafar has been teaching at the University of California, Berkeley, since 2005. He is a Dean's Teaching Fellow, lecturer and Industry Fellow at the Center of Entrepreneurship and Technology. He is also the Professor of the Practice at Brown University. He teaches courses in Entrepreneurship, Technology Strategy, Innovation and New Venture Finance at Brown and Berkeley.

Naeem is also a serial entrepreneur and currently the Founder and CEO of TeleSense, a company creating solutions in the Industrial Internet of Things (IoT) space, addressing storage and safe transport of grains. His aim is to save the food lost to bad storage conditions using technology. Previously, he co-founded and served as the CEO of Bitzer Mobile, an enterprise security and mobility company that was acquired by Oracle in 2013.

Naeem started his own business at the age of 26 and subsequently went on to start, or work at, six start-ups. His first job out of Brown University with a degree in electrical engineering was to design chips and electronic systems. Twenty years, two children, one IPO and five CEO stints later, he founded Startup-Advisor, a company focused on educating and advising entrepreneurs on all aspects of starting and running a business (www.Startup-Advisor.com).

Naeem has authored five books on entrepreneurship. These books are on topics ranging from conducting market research to seeking the right funding to finding successful ways to start a business. More information can be found on www.NaeemZafar.com. His books, including *7-Steps to a Successful Startup*, are also available on Amazon.com, Kindle and on the iTunes App store.

Acknowledgments

First and foremost, I'd like to convey my sincere gratitude to Allah, the Almighty, for every aspect of my existence. This book would not have been possible with my sole contribution. From the time I moved to Silicon Valley in December 1999 until now, I have been influenced by so many great people, both at a conscious as well as subconscious level, that it is impossible to acknowledge them all in this section – so any omissions here are purely accidental.

I have to acknowledge SAP as an organization that has given me the opportunity over the years to take risks, drive change and work with start-ups in Silicon Valley throughout the last 18 years. Without their openness and support, I would not have been able to attain the valuable experience that helped me in having the insights presented in this book.

I also would like to acknowledge SAP's Chief Design Officer, Sam Yen, whose leadership in championing Design Thinking for driving innovation has been a source of tremendous inspiration for me. Sam has also been instrumental in driving a cultural change inside SAP to become more entrepreneurial.

This book would not be possible without Janaki Kumar, a Design leader and a recognized influencer in Silicon Valley. Under Janaki's leadership, I was able to learn, grow and shine as an innovation leader.

I also would like to acknowledge Naeem Zafar, an entrepreneur and professor at UC Berkeley and Brown University, for giving me the opportunity to showcase this framework for the entrepreneurship class at UC Berkeley. Naeem also invited me to mentor start-ups during several entrepreneurial events in Silicon Valley.

Over the course of the last 15 years, I have also been able to try numerous entrepreneurial endeavors myself. My collaborators, including Bilal Ahmed, Asif Habib, Najam Saeed, Khurram Hassan and Ateeq Khan have been a great source of inspiration for me throughout these years.

I also would like to acknowledge the founders of the start-ups who asked me for my input in their endeavors. This includes Pradeep Pydah of Maxerience, Inc., and Atif Sarvari of Proge, Inc.

I would also like to thank my editor, Michael Sinocchi, and his team at Routledge/CRC Press for showing their confidence in me and exhibiting immense patience.

Finally, this book would not have been possible had my wife, Tabassum Alam, not supported and encouraged me throughout these years. Thank you very much, Tabassum, for all your love and support.

Preface

We are living in fascinating times, when the power of technology is not just reshaping but is transforming the globe in unprecedented ways. These include the ability to connect with anyone across the globe in an instant using a tiny device in the palm of our hands to the availability of self-learning systems to take over not only the most mundane of tasks but also the most sophisticated tasks previously thought to be performable only by superior human faculties.

Regardless of whether you consider this progress to be beneficial to society or harmful, these technological advancements are here to stay and will disrupt society in the future. I tend to look at these advancements from the lens of an optimist. I see these advancements as a vehicle that can unleash human potential. It has been far too long since most of us forgot our entrepreneurial roots – we traded them for a stable flow of income in the form of a paycheck at regular intervals of time. These current transformational technological advancements, on the one hand, threaten this stability, and on the other hand present an opportunity for all of us to awaken our inner entrepreneurs.

This book is an endeavor to make the transition from an employee to an entrepreneur smooth for the masses. I have not yet met a person who didn't have ideas to improve this world in some way. In fact, most of us have numerous ideas in our heads at any given moment of time and feel strongly about some of those ideas at a deeper level. However, we find ourselves perplexed on two levels:

1. Where to start to build an idea into a business?
2. What are the various dimensions and activities needed to launch an idea into a business?

This book will give you a structured approach to launching your idea into a business by following specific steps. Instead of giving a lot of theoretical concepts, this book will focus on giving an overview of the concept and specific instructions to move the idea forward.

Over the course of my 18-year career in Silicon Valley, I have driven innovation in various capacities. I have built solutions as a software developer, took solutions to market as a product manager, drove strategy for product lines as director of solution management, spearheaded an innovation-led sales program, drove numerous co-innovation and transformation engagements with the world's top enterprises in various industries, advised numerous start-ups and converted several ideas into businesses. During this time, I have been granted six US patents and won two design awards as well. I have spoken at several industry events as well as mentored numerous start-ups during many boot-camps.

As a seasoned innovation champion, I bring a unique blend of technology background, deep business expertise and design thinking skills to solve problems and help launch businesses. This experience has enabled me to see what works and what doesn't. I have captured these insights into this innovation framework that I hope will help you transform your idea into a business.

Mashhood Alam
Senior Director, Innovation and Digital Transformation
SAP Labs
Silicon Valley, CA

Chapter 1

Democratizing Entrepreneurship

With the famed stories of entrepreneurial stalwarts like Bill Gates, Steve Wozniak, Steve Jobs, Bill Hewlett and David Packard, Mark Zuckerberg, Peter Thiel, Elon Musk and the like, entrepreneurship has been perceived as the realm of elite workaholics who are passionate about their vision and achieved their vision through supernatural drive and perseverance in the face of adversity.

Although mostly grounded in some reality, that perception has also caused the masses to believe that entrepreneurship is not for all. There are two types of perspectives in this regard.

The first perspective comes from those people who are not tech savvy but have an idea of a solution to a problem they have uncovered. In some cases, they may also not have a real understanding of the problem facing a specific segment of people. However, because of their lack of understanding of technology, they tend to believe they cannot do anything with their ideas.

The other perspective comes from tech-savvy individuals who might be even working as product managers in technology companies. This perspective is based on their perception about the complexity of the process of moving their ideas from napkin to a business. Essentially, they do not know how to move their idea forward. This group also has the tendency of falling in love with the technological solution they have conceived and they do not appreciate the importance of understanding the problem first.

Both of these groups also are wary of taking risks that would subject themselves and their families to psychological stress and economic hardship.

The approach presented in this book brings together the two perspectives with the basic point of view that technology should be considered as a tool to augment human abilities, as famously quipped by Doug Engelbart, the great thought leader in the computing world.

It is time to unleash the power of human ingenuity across the globe. This structured approach of innovation should play its small part in achieving this vision.

1.1 Why Another Book on Entrepreneurship?

Over the past two decades, numerous books have been written on entrepreneurship. Some are about the author's own journey through entrepreneurship, some talk about financial and fund-raising aspects of entrepreneurial endeavors, some talk about starting a small business, some focus on building a team, others discuss marketing aspects and many discuss the accounting aspects. But none of them give a structured approach to taking an idea and then building a business.

This book provides a structured framework that anyone can use to transform their idea into a business by using principles of Design Thinking, agile development and lean start-up combined in an easy manner.

1.2 A Mind-set for Growth

One of the main reasons aspiring entrepreneurs are unable to embark on the journey of changing the world is their mind-set. As Carol Dweck recommends in her book *Mindset*, to change your mind-set from a fixed to a growth one, you should imagine what actions you will take, how you will take them and when you will take them. This book will give you a practical step-by-step approach in moving you from your idea to a business.

1.3 Basic Essence of This Innovation Approach

In today's fast-paced world, it is hard to keep up with the advancement in any field. The importance of balancing creative sparks with analytical rigor cannot be overstated. Analytical rigor focuses on leveraging new technologies to solve problems. However, creativity is required to find the problem to solve in the first place. Balancing the two sides is likely to yield the best results .

Contrary to the widely believed misconception that creativity is a result of right-brain activity and that only some blessed ones among us possess this rare trait, I have come to believe that each and every one of us is creative. However, with the passage of time and the effects of influences since our birth, first others and then we ourselves start questioning our ideas. This crushes our confidence in our creative abilities and instills doubt in our thought process.

Having experienced both the sides – the intuitive and the rational – this book connects the human-centered, design-thinking concepts with business and technology concepts. This approach takes the best from the principles of Design Thinking, a process codified by David and Tom Kelley* of IDEO[†] and Stanford D School[‡], a lean start-up model by Eric Riess and my own personal experience in driving innovation out of Silicon Valley.

In this book, I bring insights from the numerous creative engagements that I have led over the years to solve problems facing large and small companies across varying industries around the globe. The frameworks that you'll see in this book have been curated based on my real-life experiences working with large and small companies and Silicon Valley start-ups across industries that include consumer products, retail, high technology, oil and gas, manufacturing, health care, pharmaceuticals, banking, professional services, public service, automotive, transportation and semiconductors.

I hope that it will be an eye-opener for both the ones who are labeled "creative" as well as those who have enshrined their thoughts in the walls of analytical reasoning and rationality.

1.4 A Primer on Design Thinking

Before I describe the structured innovation process, it is important to give a quick overview of Design Thinking.

---

* http://www.creativeconfidence.com/authors
[†] http://www.ideo.com/
[‡] http://dschool.stanford.edu/

1.4.1 Traditional Approach

Before Design Thinking became mainstream for evaluating any business proposition, the two most important aspects that were taken into account traditionally by business executives were (1) viability, and (2) feasibility. That approach looked at the business benefits of a proposal (viability) and then evaluated whether it was doable (viability) in a financially practical manner (either through using resources of the organization or partnering with a player that could give them a speed advantage) in a timely fashion (feasibility). The initiative which ranked the highest on these two metrics was blessed with funding and kicked off. It seemed like a very reasonable way of solving problems. However, if you ask about the journey of any successful start-up, you'll realize that not a single one followed that approach. They didn't have the business value focus at the start of their venture. Nor did they have all the feasibility aspects figured out before kicking the project off. They had to go through tens and even hundreds of iterations before they could finally deliver enough value that was useful for their primary stakeholders/users. Even if you have an objective analysis of the effectiveness of that approach in established businesses, you will realize that almost all of the initiatives did not live up to their expectations.

Why did the business world continue to use that approach even if it wasn't effective? There are several reasons:

1. Both viability and feasibility are based on futuristic projections based on subjective judgments that are, in turn, based on faulty assumptions of the sponsor. Any projections by nature are fictitious and do not take into consideration the variability induced through changing parameters. These parameters are both internal as well as external.
2. The approach follows waterfall methodology* to plan for a long time, implement for an even longer time and then shove the solution down users' throats. Spending a tremendous amount of resources in planning and presenting takes precedence over recognition of assumptions and testing for validation.
3. The approach is usually compartmentalized and uses silo-ed thinking. Different teams provide their inputs from their narrow perspectives. These teams include finance, R&D, marketing, sales and operations, and they fail to recognize the interdependencies of all these disciplines.

---

* https://en.wikipedia.org/wiki/Waterfall_model

4. The approach takes time. It can be months or even years before key stakeholders see a solution. Requirements are consolidated in a spreadsheet where importance is given to the functional feature rather than the use by the user. The sponsor is fixated only on how to plan and create the corresponding features in the product to satisfy the list of requirements. This takes a long time, as all the kinks have to be straightened out on paper first so that each department can give its seal of approval before development can start. Once the scope is agreed upon, development is started, which again takes a silo-ed approach. In technology projects, the various teams work independently in building their capabilities, which are set forth in the specification document. These teams include infrastructure, database, application, user interface and integration. The final project, though it works, fails to satisfy the end users.

5. The approach is focused on "How" and "What," but rarely addresses "Why." Rather than stepping back and asking the questions such as "Why is this feature useful for the user?" or "What are the users' needs?", the focus is on "What features do we need to add?" and "How should we build the features?"

1.4.2 The New Design Thinking Approach

Design Thinking is a human-centered design approach that starts with understanding the needs of the stakeholders (desirability) and brings the viability and feasibility aspects together (Figure 1.1).

The key tenets of Design Thinking are presented next.

1.4.3 Empathy

At the heart of Design Thinking is an empathetic understanding of the user/stakeholder. It is characterized by trying to have intent observations with a childlike curiosity, not just paying attention to what the stakeholder says but paying attention to actions and actively listening to what wasn't expressed. Doing this allows you to have insights into the thoughts and feelings of users. It is easier said than done, though (Figure 1.2).

1.4.4 Have a Better Understanding of the Problem before Thinking of the Solution

Contrary to the traditional approach where the proposition starts with a solution in mind, Design Thinking is based on exploring the problem first,

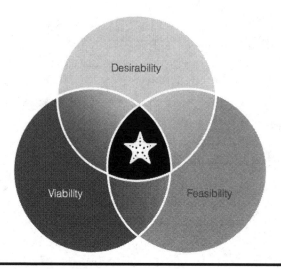

Figure 1.1 Design thinking. (Adapted from Brown, Tim. *Change By Design*. Palo Alto, CA: HarperBusiness, 2009.)

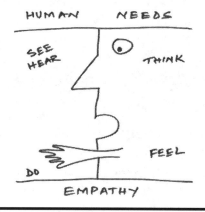

Figure 1.2 Empathy.

before even thinking about a solution. Every business starts with a hunch. The founder has an idea for the business which is generally a solution looking for a problem. Design Thinking helps explore the problem space by employing a wider lens first as the team looks from the perspective of the user, who is the main stakeholder that will benefit from the idea. To have a common understanding of the problem faced by the key user, it is important to look at the problem from different perspectives and wider lenses. This helps frame the problem from the user's context before narrowing focus on the key problem for the user.

This helps in answering the "Why" of the initiative before thinking about "How" and "What" (Figure 1.3).

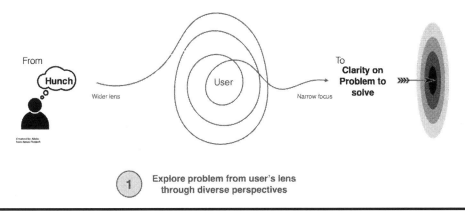

Figure 1.3 Explore the user's problem with wider lens before narrowing focus to have a clear understanding of the problem to solve.

Once the team has a clear idea of the problem, a wider lens is again used to form ideas about the various ways the problem could be solved. These ideas must take the team toward a solution which would be applicable in the user's context. As the prototypes are developed and tested with the user, the idea is further refined toward meeting the needs of the user. Through many iterations, the team not only moves closer to the solution but also has an even better understanding of the user's needs. Through this journey, the solution, which will be the "minimum viable product," will be developed and given to the user, who can then determine if the solution meets the user's needs. During this stage, the viability from the business perspective will also be taken into consideration, which will include, among other factors, the mechanism of capturing the value (pricing, channels, relationships, etc.) (Figure 1.4).

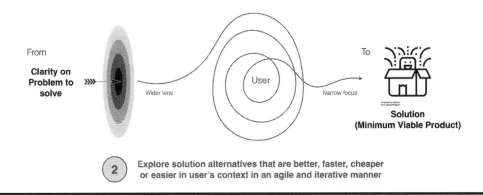

Figure 1.4 Explore solutions using wider lens before narrowing focus on specific solution ideas.

1.4.5 Collaboration with Diverse Perspectives

Design Thinking is based on the power of diverse perspectives. Getting such input means bringing key stakeholders from different lines of businesses, expertise, experience levels and backgrounds together in one room and facilitating an environment where judgments are deferred and as many ideas as possible are considered. This again highlights the importance of diversity of ideas for ideation before using convergent thinking to select the best ideas for possible solutions.

In addition, the diverse stakeholders are also brought to the same page in terms of understanding of the key stakeholders relevant for the business and the user's needs.

1.4.6 Build Prototype

Another key aspect of Design Thinking is its bias toward action. Instead of talking about the concept to death, building a prototype is required. A prototype could be as simple as a sketch on a piece of paper or as complex as a mock-up using design tools on a computer. The whole idea is that as you prototype, you see how the solution might actually be used in real life. It also reduces the need to invest tremendous resources to get user feedback.

1.4.7 Get Feedback from Target User

The beauty of this approach is its involvement of the user/key stakeholder throughout the design cycle. In this process, you do not just obtain feedback from the users on the prototype but you also involve them in coming up with ideas and doing the prototyping. In this process, you show (not tell) what a solution might look like for the users and get their feedback with an open mind.

At this point, you also obtain feedback from the business and technology/operational side to ensure the idea is both viable and feasible.

1.4.8 Iterate

And finally, be ready to fail and try again. The advantage of this approach is that you'll know fairly soon whether your process for finding a solution is moving in the right direction, unlike the traditional approach, where the user is the last person to have a glimpse at the solution.

Fail early, fail fast.

1.5 Mind-sets for Design Thinking

Design Thinking is a process that is best practiced with the following mind-sets (adapted from Stanford d.school*):

- Human-centered
- Mindful of process
- Culture of prototyping
- Show, don't tell
- Radical collaboration
- Bias toward action

1.6 Creative Leadership

The importance of believing in yourself and having the confidence to lead the creative structured process cannot be overstated throughout this approach. To successfully go through the process, you should be open to divergent thoughts, be comfortable with ambiguity because you'll be making a lot of assumptions, feel at ease at bringing diverse perspective together and use a combination of your intuition and analytic judgment to extract meaningful insights. A key aspect of creative leadership is to give yourself and your team license to fail. No endeavor of any significance has been accomplished without failure. As such, it must be considered inevitable that you will fail numerous times in your journey before achieving success.

1.7 Best Way to Get the Best out of This Approach

Working on your idea requires focused effort. This approach will help you remain focused through an 18-step structured process spread across four stages that you can complete within six to twelve weeks.

1.7.1 Build a Team

You are not likely to be working alone in this endeavor, so think about building a core team of two to five members who would be working

---

* http://dschool.stanford.edu/

together on the project. While building the team, consider the following aspects:

- *Trust*: This is the single most important aspect of any team's success. Without trust between team members, no idea would see the light of day.
- *Positive attitude*: You do not want people who are skeptics or who drain your energy by pointing out how an idea could fail. Build a team with members who are upbeat about the topic and possess a "can do" attitude.
- *Skills*: You should look for members who bring complementary skills and experiences to the team so you could build on each other's ideas.
- *Personal chemistry*: Finally, you need to build a team with whom you can hang out and spend hours at a stretch without getting bored.

1.7.2 Review the Framework with the Team

Make sure every member of your team reads through all the steps in this framework and discuss their perspectives as a group.

1.7.3 Collaborative Engagement

I recommend gathering in one room as you work on your idea. Have a whiteboard or flip chart easel with an easel pad, a set of sticky notes and pens or markers to capture thoughts as you work through the framework.

In certain cases, you'll realize that you already have insights about a specific topic. In those cases, just share your insights with the team and ensure that everyone is on the same page. You'll be surprised to find at every step of this framework how much you assumed about the problem and how varied are the insights from different team members.

1.7.4 Capture Assumptions

Pay close attention to all the assumptions you are making at every step of this framework, and make sure you record these assumptions in one place. These assumptions help you focus on activities that are most important to move your idea forward. These assumptions also help you recognize the risk inherent in your idea.

1.7.5 Guidance

As you work on each step in this framework, you'll need to follow a few principles of brainstorming. These include:

- *Give time for self-brainstorming.* Different members have different personality traits. Some are more extroverted and get their energy from other people. Some are intrinsically introverted and get a boost in energy when they are in isolation. You need to ensure ideas from all the individuals in your team are extracted and discussed. Self-brainstorming allows the latter group enough opportunity to think about and share their ideas.
- *Document every thought on sticky notes.* Divergent ideas often yield amazing results. However, if the ideas are not captured, discussed and contemplated, they tend to disappear and diffuse sooner than we realize. So it is imperative that you ensure ideas from the team are captured in a structured manner. If you are brainstorming in a room, capture these ideas on sticky notes or any other medium that works for your team.
- *Defer judgment.* Since the time of our birth, we have all been subjected to judgments by others. As a child begins to take his/her first steps, parents jump in to save them or warn them of falling (failing). As the child grows up to imagine a new world, the culture or school system puts boundaries of conformity on his/her ideas. In school, we are trained in critical thinking –closely examining ideas – and following rules. Throughout this journey, we start internalizing these judgments and start judging and questioning our own thoughts and ideas subconsciously. Never pass judgment on your own and others' ideas.
- *Allow every member to share and describe their thoughts.* Another pitfall that we all fall into is this: as soon as we have an idea, we tend to stick to it and consider that it is the best idea put forth by the entire team. We tend to overlook, dismiss or never listen to ideas from others. Ensure that you pay close attention to ideas, regardless of where they are coming from.
- *Allow one person to speak at one time.* In the excitement of the moment, we also fall into the trap of overpowering others and squelching their voice unintentionally. Ensure that you don't speak over each other.

- *Build on each other's ideas.* Finally, don't be shy in connecting different ideas together to have better insights and solutions. Creativity is nothing but taking ideas from one domain and applying to another.

Throughout this book, you'll find instructions on how to run the corresponding brainstorming session for each step. You'll need to dedicate one person from the team as the "lead" for the brainstorming session who will facilitate the session and have the team members contribute and discuss.

Chapter 2

The Three Stages Plus One

This framework is grounded in the belief that all solutions solve human problems and strive to augment human capabilities by introducing a new way of doing things using technology or otherwise (Figure 2.1).

The framework is divided into the following four stages:

STAGE 1: UNDERSTAND THE PROBLEM to have a clear idea of the desirability by key stakeholder(s).

STAGE 2: DEVISE A SOLUTION to determine feasibility of the new approach.

STAGE 3: CRAFT BUSINESS to get an insight into viability from business perspective.

As you go through each stage, you'll be making lots of assumptions. These assumptions are the key driver for the risk in the pursuit and must be validated as the team continues to work on the idea. Which leads to the fourth stage:

STAGE 4: MANAGE RISK to have honest recognition of the inherent uncertainty, a key ingredient of any new pursuit.

It is important to note that, although this framework walks you through the above four stages in a sequential order, you can start from any of the first three stages of the framework and go in any direction.

For example, you may already have an idea of a technological solution in mind. So you'd go to the second stage (Devise Solution). However, as you will see, it will soon be evident to you that you need to go back to the first stage (understand problem) to have a clear understanding of

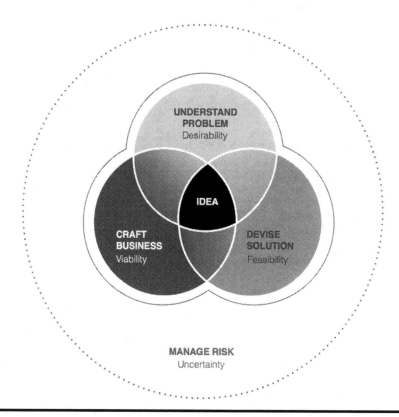

Figure 2.1   The four stages of transforming an idea into a business.

the stakeholders who have a problem that your solution is trying to solve. In other cases, you might have an idea of a new business model to apply in an existing context. As you go through the third stage (craft business), you'll find the need to go to the first and the second stages to understand the value proposition you are trying to articulate for specific stakeholders through a novel solution. And remember, throughout your journey, you will be making lots and lots of assumptions in all aspects of your venture. This will require you to go to stage 4 (manage risk) frequently.

2.1 Let Your Curiosity Drive Your Endeavor

Endeavors of significance help answer important questions. Through the course of your pursuit, this framework will help you ask the questions that you should ask yourself and try to find answer for. These answers will help you move your idea forward. Remember that as you'll find answers to these questions, your idea is likely to morph and evolve so much that it would not look quite like what you had in mind when you started this journey. Do not be alarmed! This is the right way to go about transforming your idea into a business. Here are some of the questions that you'll be asking yourself as you go forward.

2.1.1 Questions for the First Stage

In the first stage, the most important questions are as follows:

1. Who is the target stakeholder (or target user) who will benefit from your idea?
2. What problem does your idea solve?
3. What is the current way the user solves this problem?
4. What is the job the user needs to do?
5. What is the goal the user is looking to achieve?
6. Is there a vision that the user is wishing to realize?
7. What is the current end-to-end experience or journey that the user has to go through to complete the job your idea will help with?
8. What are the systems, tools and people that the user relies on to do the job today?
9. What is the emotional state of your target user during his/her current experience?
10. What are the main pain points a user encounters today?
11. Why is the job important for the user to do?
12. What are the user's contextual elements that need to be taken into consideration?
13. What does the user see in his/her context where your idea will be used?
14. What are the target user's thinking and feelings in the current situation?
15. Who are the other stakeholders connected with the user?
16. How will the connected stakeholders benefit from your solution?
17. How will the connected stakeholders be impacted by your solution?
18. How will the connected stakeholders impact the usage of your solution?
19. Who are the other stakeholders influenced by or actively influencing the target user?
20. Could the influenced stakeholders play a role in aiding/hindering adoption of your solution?
21. Are there other stakeholders who could benefit from your idea?

2.1.2 Questions for the Second Stage

In the second stage, the most important questions are as follows:

1. What are the other ways this problem could be solved?
2. How feasible is it to build the solution to address the user's needs?
3. What would be the new end-to-end experience for the user if your idea is implemented?
4. How can you prototype without investing too much time and money?
5. How can you test your idea with the user today?
6. What system, tool and people will the user need to rely upon in the new experience?
7. Does the solution help the user hit the target (complete the job, achieve the goal or realize the vision) in a better, cheaper, faster or easier way?
8. Why would the user change the current way of doing the job and adopt the new experience?
9. Are the benefits of the new approach significant enough to entice the user to adopt the new approach?
10. How could you influence the user in adopting the new experience?
11. Are there any personal motivations or behaviors that would help the user see the value in the new approach?
12. Are there any social elements that would help the user adopt the new approach?
13. Are there any structural elements that would help the user adopt the new approach?
14. Are there any implications or reliance on other stakeholders in the new experience?
15. Are there any implications or reliance on existing/other processes in the organization?
16. Are there any implications or reliance on other data sources or systems?

2.1.3 Questions for the Third Stage

Key questions in the third stage include:

1. What are the short- and long-term industry trends which would help or hinder adoption of your idea?
2. What are the short- and long-term technology trends which would help or hinder adoption of your idea?

3. What are the short- and long-term business model trends which would help or hinder adoption of your idea?
4. What are the short- and long-term macroeconomic trends which would help or hinder adoption of your idea?
5. What are the short- and long-term demographic trends which would help or hinder adoption of your idea?
6. Who are the current and future competitors for your business? Competitors include other players as well as the current way to doing the job.
7. How will the user (and market) know about your business?
8. How will you deliver value to your customers?
9. What kind of relationship will you need to have with your users?
10. What resources (skills and assets) do you need to build your solution?
11. What processes (activities and capabilities) do you need to do to create the value for your user?
12. Which technologies would you need to use to create your solution?
13. Which partners would you need to rely upon in any aspect of value creation and delivery for your business?
14. How will you capture the value generated from your venture?
15. What will be your pricing strategy?
16. How will you get paid?
17. When will you get paid for the value delivery?
18. How will you fund the venture?

2.1.4 Questions for the Fourth Stage

The two key questions here are:

1. Throughout each step in all the stages in this framework, what are you assuming to hold true to make your idea work?
2. How could you test and validate your assumptions?

2.2 Failing Early, and Failing Fast

One of the main concepts underpinning this book is for you to recognize that having an emotional attachment to your idea might lead to a myopic view of the world. That way of looking at the world is highlighted by the age-old maxim, "To the one with a hammer in hand, every problem looks like a nail." Although entrepreneurship is inherently about risk taking, successful entrepreneurs are pragmatic risk managers. Throughout the journey, you and your team must have honest recognition of the uncertainty inherent in your venture. You must evaluate whether your idea is viable from a business perspective and feasible to implement.

Instead of continuing to beat a dead horse, this framework will also help you have that honest insight to fail early and fail fast.

You only fail when you try your ideas with relevant stakeholders and test your assumptions. So regardless of which stage you are focusing on, you must be testing your assumptions with key stakeholders. You'll learn about how to prototype and test your ideas in the second stage of this framework. However, you may use the same tools and mind-set to prototype and test not just your solution ideas but also your understanding of the user problem or any aspect of the business model as well.

2.3 The Problem Statement

Before you start working on the first stage, write down a problem statement that describes the problem you are trying to solve or the question you are trying to find an answer for.

The problem statement clearly describes two aspects:

What problem are you solving, and for whom?

The problem statement acts a guiding light for you and your team. "Template 1 The Challenge or Problem Statement" below shows you how to write a problem statement.

2.3.1 Template

Describe your problem statement on the following template (Figure 2.2):

2.3.2 Example

Some of the examples of a problem statement are as follows (Figure 2.3):

How might we _____?

How do we _____ _____ to _____?

Figure 2.2 The challenge or problem statement.

How might we help project managers of non-profit organizations in urban centers to plan and execute philanthropic projects?

How do we enable quality managers to run more tests in a lab environment?

How might we help project managers for non-profit organizations in urban counties in America to plan and manage projects?

How might we instill love of STEM in middle school kids in impoverished communities through games?

How might we enable stay-home moms who love cooking to sell their cuisines to working professionals who do not have time to cook and wish to eat home cooked meals?

Figure 2.3   The challenge or problem statement examples.

2.3.3 Guidance

2.3.3.1 Session Lead

Write "How might we" on a flip chart or whiteboard and ask participants to complete the phrase to convey the problem definition.

Convey that the problem statement should:

■ Not be too broad as to "boil the ocean," or, for example, "How might we solve world hunger?"
■ Not be too narrow as to "direct to a potential solution," or, for example, "How might we deliver hot lunches to homeless people via motorcycle in front of the city center by collecting extra food from restaurants?"
■ Have a right level somewhere in the middle. For example, "How might we fulfill daily nutritional needs for hungry people in the downtown area?"
■ Highlight the problem and the key stakeholder who has the problem.
■ Not hint toward any potential solution, for example, "How might we build a mobile app to link nonprofit organizations to donors?"

2.3.3.2 Three-minute Self-brainstorm

All participants think of a different version of the problem statement without talking with each other and each writes one problem statement per sticky note.

2.3.3.3 Team Brainstorm

Session lead asks each participant to come to the flip chart/whiteboard, place the statements and explain their statement to the team.

Once all the statements are placed on the wall, the team should discuss and agree on one problem statement. This statement should build on the various versions and may also combine several statements into one. Expect several iterations before a consensus is reached.

2.3.3.4 Document Assumptions

After agreeing on the problem statement, the session lead should ask the team to write down all the assumptions that you are making and record those assumptions in the assumptions template in Chapter 6.

2.4 Overview of the Transform^{3+1} Framework

Before we delve into the details of each of the stages, let's walk through the framework, which I call "Transform^{3+1}," on a high level (Figure 2.4).

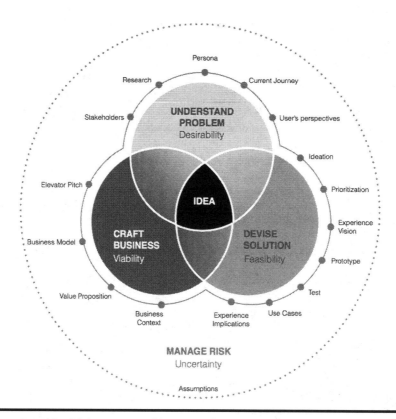

Figure 2.4 Transform^{3+1} Framework to transform ideas into business with design thinking.

In stage 1, you'll develop a deep understanding of the stakeholders relevant for your idea and do user research to develop personas and capture their current journey. This will allow you to develop an insightful point of view for the key stakeholder or stakeholders who have a problem that your idea intends to solve.

Stage 2 will walk you through the ideation techniques, building future experience vision, prototypes and testing of your prototypes with key stakeholders. You'll be able to recognize the importance of not being emotionally tied to the first idea you had for a solution and of listening to the customer and testing your ideas without investing too much of your time and resources in finalizing the solution offering. This will also help you understand the use cases for which the solution will be beneficial for the stakeholders as well as recognize dependencies of the future experience on existing processes, in case the solution is geared toward enterprises.

In stage 3, you'll convert your use cases into a value proposition and have a better understanding of the complexities involved in converting an idea into a business model in a complex world full of competitors and other trends that have an impact on how you go to market with your solution. These complexities include financial implications, resources, activities and partnerships needed and channel to reach customers.

Finally, throughout the above three stages, you and your team must be documenting all the assumptions you are making, which will help you have an honest insight into the uncertainty inherent in your venture. In this stage, you'll be able to manage risk as you pursue your endeavor.

It is important to highlight at this stage, as indicated in the circular Venn diagrammatic depiction of the framework, that as you work through this framework, you will be going back and forth between the various steps of the framework. When you are focusing on one stage, you may follow the steps therein sequentially. However, you should feel open to jumping to a different stage and step to brainstorm and come back to the step you were working on afterward. The sequence of the framework is provided to guide your thinking primarily and should not be considered as a step-by-step process that has to be followed strictly.

Chapter 3

Stage 1: Understand Problem to Grasp Desirability

The first stage is the most important stage of any endeavor. It is the crux of your endeavor. This stage will help you have a clear vision as to WHY your idea is important and WHO the primary beneficiary of your solution is. Answers to questions raised in this stage help in setting the vision and rationale behind your quest. Unless you have a clear idea of who the stakeholders are for whom you are solving a problem and what those problems are, it is impossible to envision a solution that would benefit the stakeholders.

By following the subsequent steps, you will develop a solid understanding of why the problem is worth solving. That is, the "desirability" of solving the problem for the user.

3.1 Step 1: Stakeholders

The first step is to have a clear understanding of the stakeholders involved around your problem statement. Stakeholders are all the persons who would be the direct beneficiaries of your solution or would be directly or indirectly affected by your idea. Think about the people who have a problem that you are solving, or those who would be paying for the solution or who will be directly or indirectly impacted by the problem you have identified or the solution that you would propose. All those are stakeholders for your idea.

Using the "Template 2 Stakeholders Map," identify all the core, direct and indirect stakeholders for your idea.

3.1.1 Target Stakeholders

Target stakeholders are the primary beneficiaries of your idea. Identify minimum of one and maximum of three core stakeholders who will also be the users of your solution.

3.1.2 Connected Stakeholders

Connected stakeholders are all the stakeholders who are connected to the target users and are thereby directly influencing or being influenced by your target users in the context of your idea. These are also the stakeholders who might be paying or helping implement the solution that you'll be envisioning. Note that in many cases, the one who pays for the solution may not necessarily be the one who uses it. And the one who implements the solution may be a totally different person.

3.1.3 Influenced Stakeholders

Influenced stakeholders are all other identified stakeholders who influence or are indirectly influenced by your target users or connected stakeholders. The reason to think of all the connected and influenced stakeholders is to have an exploratory approach to the problem space and not look at the problem space only through the narrow lens of identified target stakeholders.

3.1.4 Stakeholder Template (Figure 3.1)

Here is one example of stakeholders if your problem statement is:

> *How might we enable stay-at-home moms who love cooking to sell their cuisines to working professionals who do not have time to cook and wish to eat home-cooked meals?* (Figure 3.2)

In this case, target stakeholders could be *stay-at-home moms, aunts, dads, grandparents and working professionals.*

Connected stakeholders could be *family members, neighbors for the cook and co-workers for the working professionals.*

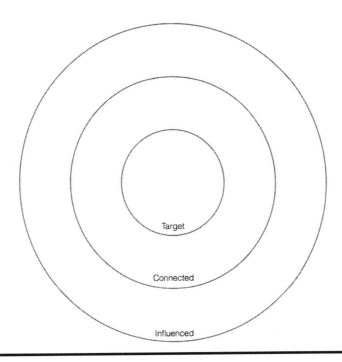

Figure 3.1   Stakeholders.

Influenced stakeholders could be *homeowners' association managers, local regulators, grocery stores, vegetable providers, meat providers, professional kitchen providers and others.*

3.1.5 Guidance

3.1.5.1 Session Lead

Draw the template on a flip chart/whiteboard.

Ask participants to identify all stakeholders who:

- Have a problem that you are solving.
- Are the primary users/beneficiaries of your solution.
- Could benefit in any other domain, function or industry. (Thinking about beneficiaries in domains other than the one you are thinking of directly also helps in stirring up new ideas of applicability of your solution.)
- Will pay for the solution. (Buyer may be different than the user.)
- Will implement the solution. (Is there another stakeholder who will make the solution ready for use?)

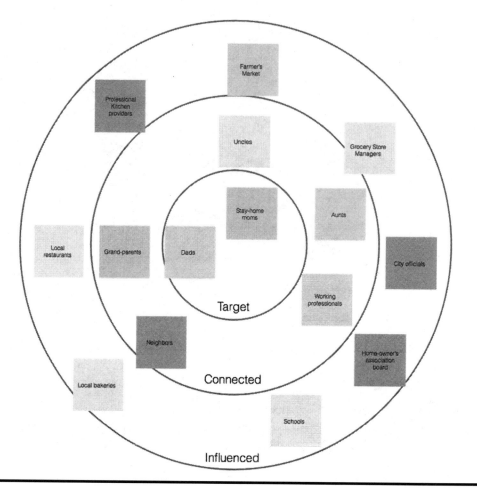

Figure 3.2   Stakeholders example.

- Are directly impacted by primary users of your solution.
- Are indirectly impacted by primary users or your solution.

3.1.5.2 Three-minute Self-brainstorm

All participants think of the stakeholders without talking with each other. All participants write one stakeholder name per sticky note.

3.1.5.3 Team Brainstorm

The facilitator asks each participant to place the stakeholders one by one and places the stakeholders in the appropriate category (target, connected and influenced).

The team should come to a consensus on the stakeholders and their placement on the template. The team should also identify at least one and no more than three target stakeholders for the problem space. We also call them users.

3.1.5.4 Document Assumptions

After agreeing on the stakeholders, the session lead should ask the team to write down all the assumptions that you are making and record those assumptions in the assumptions template in Chapter 6.

3.1.5.5 Review Prior Steps

At this point, it is suggested to review the problem statement to ensure it is still valid. Adjust the problem statement as needed with the consensus of the team.

3.2 Step 2: Research

Many entrepreneurs jump into solving the problems from day one without adequately understanding the needs of the primary beneficiary of the imagined solution, the context in which the user operates, the wider context, including competitive options, behavioral trends, technology trends, industry trends and other relevant aspects.

Spending some time in conducting research about these aspects will help guide your thinking in the right direction. Research also gives you valuable insights into the needs of the users.

Business Context in step 13 will guide you through the macro context in which you are operating. In this step, you'll focus on the core user and how to research to uncover real needs of the user.

User research is "the single most" important aspect of any project. If done right, you are likely to uncover insights that will enable you to address real needs of the user. The main objective of research is to "empathize" with the users/core stakeholders. There are three important aspects of user research:

1. Planning
2. Observation
3. Engagement

3.2.1 Planning

Before you go out for user research, it is important to plan the research. Think about all the avenues of primary and secondary research. Primary research entails directly observing and interviewing the users. Secondary research includes finding out information from other sources, including online, other people who would know the space better, books, library and media.

For primary research, you need to find and narrow down where to find the users to observe and research. The best approach is, if you already know people in this space, to reach out to them directly. Otherwise, find out ways to reach out to the users and explain why you need their time and how the research will help you in understanding their needs better.

3.2.2 Empathetic Observation

Observation pertains to viewing users and their behavior in the context of their lives/work. Watching what people do and how they interact with their environment gives you clues about what they think and feel. It helps you to learn about what they need. By watching people, you can capture physical manifestations of their experiences, what they do and say. This will allow you to interpret the intangible meaning of those experiences in order to uncover insights. These insights will lead you to innovative solutions. The best solutions come out of the best insights into human behavior.

But learning to recognize those insights is harder than you might think, because our minds automatically filter out a lot of information in ways we aren't even aware of. We need to learn to see things "with a fresh set of eyes." Tools for empathy, along with a human-centered mind-set, are what gives us those new eyes.

3.2.3 Genuine Curiosity

To have genuine curiosity, you must engage with users through empathetic questioning. Think of it as personally connecting with someone rather than interviewing or surveying someone. This mind-set allows you to seek the deeper insights and ask the harder questions. At the end of your time with a user, you want to have captured what that person said and did, and you want to have an understanding of what that person thinks and feels.

3.2.4 Being Inquisitive Is Good, Without Being Intrusive!

We want to understand a person's experience as a user in the space so that we can determine how to innovate for him/her. By understanding the choices that person makes and the behaviors that person engages in, we can identify needs and design for these needs. Use this map to guide your interview:

- Introduce yourself and your team.
- Introduce the project and explain why you are doing the research.
- Build rapport.
- Do not go through the interview questionnaire question by question. Instead, have the questionnaire as a guide and have the engagement as a conversation.
- Listen to the user responses intently to understand rather than rushing to finish asking all the questions.

3.2.5 Adopt a Beginner's Mind-set

We all carry our experiences, understanding and expertise with us. These aspects of yourself are incredibly valuable assets to bring to the design challenge – but at the right time, and with intentionality. Your assumptions may be misconceptions and stereotypes, and they can restrict the amount of real empathy you can build. Assume a beginner's mind-set in order to put aside these biases so that you can approach a design challenge with fresh eyes. Be mindful of the following aspects:

3.2.6 Don't Judge

Just observe and engage users without the influence of value judgments upon their actions, circumstances, decisions or "issues."

3.2.7 Question Everything

Question even (and especially) the things you think you already understand. Ask questions to learn about how the user perceives the world. Think about how a four-year-old asks "Why?" about everything. Follow up an answer to one "why" with a second "why."

3.2.8 Be Genuinely Curious

Strive to assume a posture of wonder and curiosity, especially in circumstances that seem either familiar or uncomfortable.

3.2.9 Find Patterns

Look for interesting threads, patterns and themes that emerge across interactions with users.

3.2.10 Listen, Intently

Lose your agenda and let the scene soak into your psyche. Absorb what users say to you, and how they say it, without thinking about the next thing you're going to say.

3.2.11 Suggestions for User Engagement

Ask why. Even when you think you know the answer, ask people why they do or say things. The answers will sometimes surprise you.

Encourage stories. Whether or not the stories people tell are true, they reveal how they think about the world. Ask questions that get people telling stories.

Look for inconsistencies. Sometimes what people say and what they do are different. These inconsistencies often hide interesting insights.

Listen to nonverbal cues. Be aware of body language and emotions.

Don't be afraid of silence. Interviewers often feel the need to ask another question when there is a pause. Sometimes if you allow there to be silence, a person will reflect on what they've just said and say something deeper.

Don't suggest answers to your questions. Even if they pause before answering, don't help them by suggesting an answer. This can unintentionally get people to say things that agree with your expectations.

Ask questions neutrally. "What do you think about this idea?" is a better question than "Don't you think this idea is great?" because the first question doesn't imply that there is a right answer. Don't offer approval or disapproval with words, facial expressions or body language.

3.2.12 Engagement Guidelines with the User

Prepare a list of questions before the interview.

Two to three people should go for the engagement.

The team should be prepped on the engagement model and preferably trained on empathy-based engagements.

The team should interview three or more users in the same role and synthesize those insights afterward.

It is recommended to assign a dedicated interviewer and note taker for user research.

3.2.12.1 Guidelines for Interviewer

- One person should take the role of interviewer who will drive the questioning.
- Ask open-ended questions.
- Review the guidelines mentioned above.
- Do not go through the interview questionnaire question by question. Instead, have the questionnaire as a guide and have the engagement as a conversation.
- Listen to the user responses intently to understand rather than rushing to finish asking all the questions.

3.2.12.2 Guidelines for Note Taker

- Other person(s) should be solely responsible for taking notes.
- Only ask questions for clarification.
- Use the "Observation Template" and "Note-Taking Template" to record the observations and answers.
- Take pictures of the surroundings and the user with his/her permission.
- Review the guidelines mentioned above.

3.2.12.3 Sample Questions for Interview

Sample questions for an enterprise engagement include the following:

1. Introduction:
   a. Tell me about yourself.
   b. What is your educational background?
   c. How long have you been in this role?
   d. What did you do before this job?
2. Jobs to be done:
   a. Tell me about your role.
   b. What are your responsibilities?
   c. Who is your manager, and how does he/she measure your performance?
   d. How do you fulfill your responsibilities today?
   e. Whom do you rely on to do your job?
      i. Which other people within and outside your team?
      ii. Which information do you rely on?
      iii. How do you get that information?
      iv. Do you know how this information was generated/aggregated?
      v. Do you trust the information?
      vi. How soon do you see that information?
      vii. What do you do with that information?
      viii. Do you massage the information in a certain way yourself to have a better understanding of the reality?
      ix. Can you show us how you do that?
      x. Can you show us how you see the information today?
   f. What decisions do you have to make daily/weekly/monthly/quarterly/yearly?
   g. Whom do you interact with to make your decisions?
   h. How much of the decision making is subjective, based on your experience?
   i. How would someone with much less experience than you have make such decisions?
   j. How do you know that the decisions that you made had a positive or negative impact?
   k. Can you walk us through the major tasks you do? We'd just shadow you and make observations and ask questions to have a better understanding of your challenges.

3. Customers:
   a. Who are your customers?
   b. Tell me more about your customers – are they both internal and external?
   c. What do these customers expect of you?
   d. What are their biggest challenges?
   e. What is the job that you are helping your customer do?
   f. How else can your customers do their job if you did not provide the product/service?
4. Challenges:
   a. What are your biggest challenges?
   b. Why are you facing these challenges?
   c. How many of these challenges are related to organization?
   d. How many of these challenges are related to processes?
   e. How many of these challenges are related to technology?
5. Aspirations:
   a. In an ideal world, how would you be doing your job?
   b. What are the factors that you would like to maximize in your job?
   c. How would you solve the challenges you identified earlier on?
6. Evoke stories throughout the interview:
   a. Tell me about a time when … ?
      i. Tell me about a time when things didn't go as planned?
      ii. Tell me about a time when things worked better than expected?
7. Understand emotions:
   a. How did you feel when this happened?
   b. Tell me more about how you felt at that point?
8. Conclusion:
   a. Thank the user for his/her time.
   b. Tell the user about the next steps:
      i. What you will do with all this information and when they can expect to hear some progress on the research.
      ii. You'll be interviewing other users as well.
      iii. You'll be synthesizing this information.
      iv. You'll be coming back to them for validation.
      v. You'll be thinking about new ways to do things/solutions.
      vi. You'll be inviting them for their input on new solutions.
      vii. You'll be prototyping new solutions and sharing them with users to get feedback.

viii. You'll be prioritizing use cases across all verticals.
  ix. You'll be building solutions for them if their area was selected as the top use case.
  c. Thank them again for their time and openness.

3.2.13 Template

Capture your insights on the following template, from observation to interpretation and deriving insights (Figure 3.3).

Bring notes back from the engagement and complete the Template 4 Empathy Map.

Name	Other relevant demographic information
Gender	
Age	
Education Level	

Observation

What does the user see?	What does the user hear?
What does the user say?	What does the user do?

Interpretations

What does the user think?	How does the user feel?

Insights

What does the user need?	What are user's key challenges?

Figure 3.3   Empathy template.

3.2.14 Example (Figure 3.4)

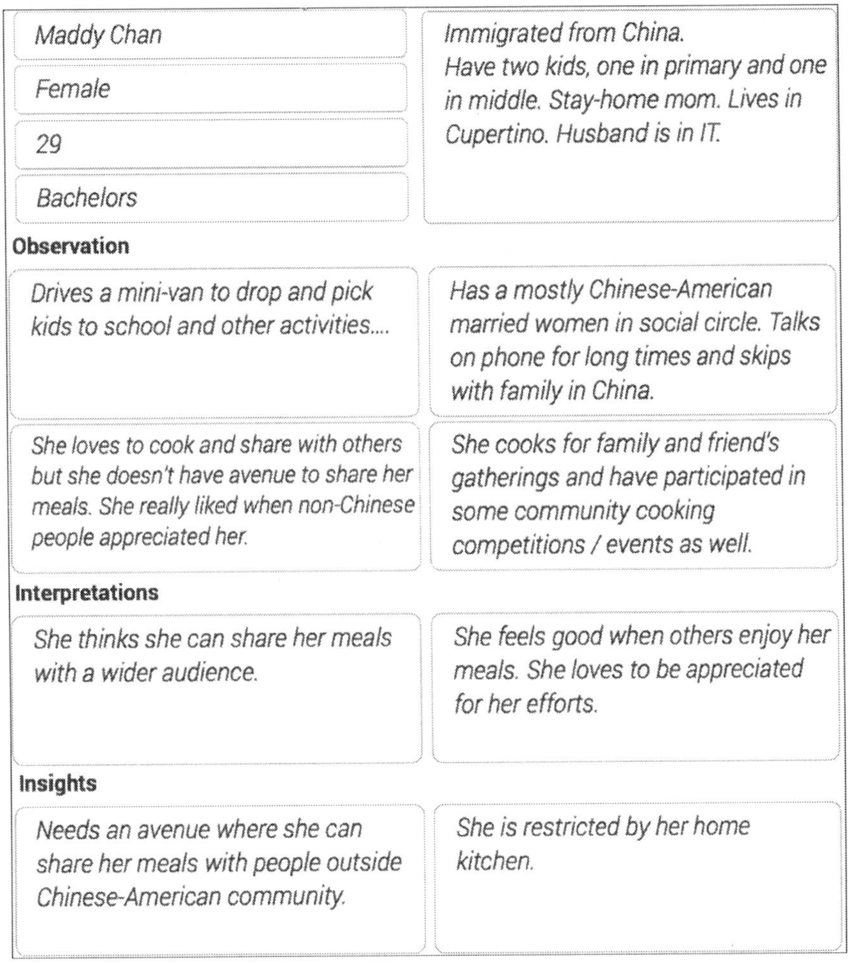

Maddy Chan Female 29 Bachelors	Immigrated from China. Have two kids, one in primary and one in middle. Stay-home mom. Lives in Cupertino. Husband is in IT.

Observation

Drives a mini-van to drop and pick kids to school and other activities....	Has a mostly Chinese-American married women in social circle. Talks on phone for long times and skips with family in China.
She loves to cook and share with others but she doesn't have avenue to share her meals. She really liked when non-Chinese people appreciated her.	She cooks for family and friend's gatherings and have participated in some community cooking competitions / events as well.

Interpretations

She thinks she can share her meals with a wider audience.	She feels good when others enjoy her meals. She loves to be appreciated for her efforts.

Insights

Needs an avenue where she can share her meals with people outside Chinese-American community.	She is restricted by her home kitchen.

Figure 3.4   Empathy example.

3.2.14.1 Guidance

Session Lead

For each user research, draw the template on a flip chart/whiteboard. Use one color of sticky notes for each user interviewed (do not mix colors).

Ask participants to record their research in this template:

Observations

- What was the user doing?
- What was the user uttering/saying?
- What was the user seeing?
- What was his/her environment?

Interpretations and/or answers

- What are the user's thoughts?
- What are the user's feelings?

Insights

- What are user needs and challenges?

10-minute self-brainstorm

- All participants document their user research insights on sticky notes.

3.2.14.2 Team Brainstorm

The session lead asks everyone to come to the flipchart and paste their thoughts.

All Users

Repeat the brainstorming session for all the users researched. Use different color sticky notes for recording research insights from each user.

Synthesize

Ask everyone to bring insights from the different users into one empathy map. The team should be able to see common themes emerging across different users as well as unique insights from individual users. These insights should be discussed in order to further develop empathy with the user and generate ideas.

3.2.14.3 Document Assumptions

After the session, the session lead should ask the team to write down all the assumptions that you are making and record those assumptions in the assumptions template in Chapter 6.

3.3 Step 3: Persona

Persona is a fictitious representation of the main user who would be using your product or service. Bring the insights from user research to life and build a fictitious persona for each of your core users.

3.3.1 Template

Use this template to build your user's persona (Figure 3.5).

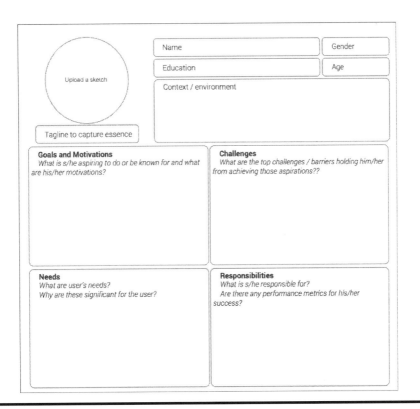

Figure 3.5 Persona template.

3.3.2 Example

Here is an example of a persona for a user (Figure 3.6).

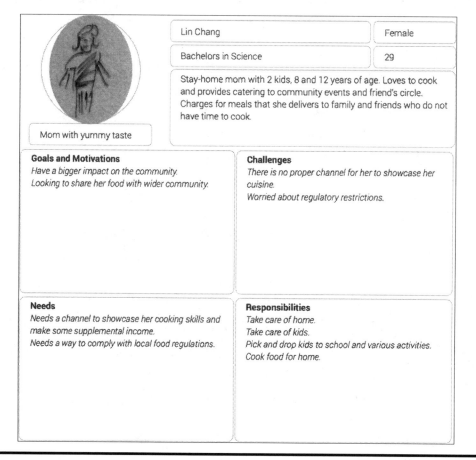

| Lin Chang | Female |
| Bachelors in Science | 29 |

Stay-home mom with 2 kids, 8 and 12 years of age. Loves to cook and provides catering to community events and friend's circle. Charges for meals that she delivers to family and friends who do not have time to cook.

Mom with yummy taste

Goals and Motivations
Have a bigger impact on the community.
Looking to share her food with wider community.

Challenges
There is no proper channel for her to showcase her cuisine.
Worried about regulatory restrictions.

Needs
Needs a channel to showcase her cooking skills and make some supplemental income.
Needs a way to comply with local food regulations.

Responsibilities
Take care of home.
Take care of kids.
Pick and drop kids to school and various activities.
Cook food for home.

Figure 3.6 Persona example.

3.3.2.1 Guidance

Session Lead

As a team, give this persona a name. Agree on the age, gender and education level.

10-minute self-brainstorm

Give everyone 10 minutes to put their thoughts on sticky notes to capture the following aspects for the persona:

- Goals and motivation in the context of your idea.
- Challenges faced to achieve these goals.
- Primary responsibilities for the persona in the context of your idea.
- Needs.

Team Brainstorm

The session lead asks everyone to come to the flip chart and paste their thoughts.

After all the team members have shared out, cluster the input and agree on the key aspects of the persona so that the whole team is on the same page.

Draw a sketch that represents the persona and give a creative tag line that captures the essence of the persona. Have some fun while doing this exercise.

All Users

Repeat the brainstorming session for all the users for your idea. Build one persona for each user segment.

From now on, every time you discuss the users, use the persona's name so that everyone on your team would have the same visual picture in their minds and have a similar understanding of the needs and context of the core user for your idea.

3.3.2.2 Document Assumptions

After the session, the session lead should ask the team to write down all the assumptions that you are making and record those assumptions in the assumptions template in Chapter 6.

3.3.2.3 Review Prior Steps

Review the prior steps and adjust as needed with the consensus of the team.

3.4 Step 4: Current Journey

To understand the user's perspective and be in his/her shoes, build the customer journey in the context of your idea. The goal is to have a holistic and comprehensive understanding of the user's context and build empathy with the user. Depending on the situation, you may sketch multiple customer journeys for each persona.

3.4.1 Current Journey Template

Document current journey in the following template (Figure 3.7).

Figure 3.7   Current journey template.

3.4.2 Current Journey Example (Figure 3.8)

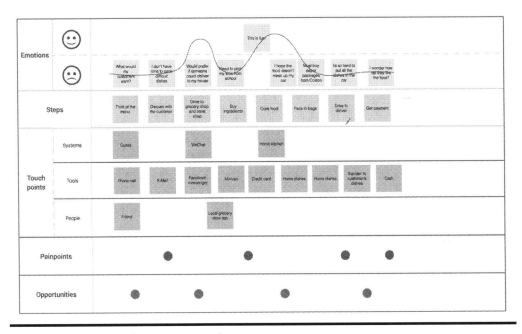

Figure 3.8   Current journey example.

3.4.2.1 Guidance

Session Lead

Ask the team to write all the steps the user does in his/her journey.

- List the steps the user takes in the context of the problem space.
- For each step, identify touch points, which are systems, resources and people that the user relies upon to perform that step.
- Then go through the user's emotional state of mind while performing each step.
- Give red and green voting dots to participants and ask them to highlight pain points and moments of truth.
- "Moments of truth" are the points where the user is most susceptible to emotional influence.

Use different colored sticky notes for steps, touch points and emotions.

As you complete the journey map, go through the emotions and draw a line to depict highs and lows from users' emotional aspects.

15-minute Self-brainstorm

Give everyone on your team fifteen minutes to jot down thoughts for steps, touch points and emotions for each user.

Team Brainstorm

Everyone comes to the board and explains each sticky note as they paste it on the wall.

The team should review the steps, touch points and emotions and move sticky notes around to reflect the journey of the user.

Use a marker to traverse the emotional state of the user throughout the journey to highlight the emotional journey of the user as well.

Once the journey map steps, touch points and emotions are completed, hand over red dots and green dots to each team member. Everyone should place red dots on sticky notes to indicate pain points for the user and green dots to indicate "moments of truth" for the user. Paint points are, as the name suggests, difficulties that the user encounters while going through the journey. "Moments of truth" are the points where the user is emotionally vulnerable. In other words, these are the points where you could influence the user the most.

Put yourself into the user's shoes and walk through this journey to build empathy with the user.

3.4.2.2 Document Assumptions

After the session, the session lead should ask the team to write down all the assumptions that you are making and record those assumptions in the assumptions template in Chapter 6. In case there are disagreements about any aspect of the user journey, make an assumption of the most likely scenario and document that assumption in the assumptions section as well.

3.4.2.3 Review Prior Steps

Review the prior steps and adjust as needed with the consensus of the team.

3.5 Step 5: User's Perspective

The user's point of view is a critical step in having a solid understanding of the problem you are trying to solve. The point of view is deeper than a statement summarizing the needs. It is full of insights that can only be extracted if you have really built empathy for the user. This is the opportunity to capture those nuggets of insights which form the basis of your idea. Craft these points of view in the following form:

User X needs a way to do a job because insight.

3.5.1 Template

Capture user's perspective in the following template (Table 3.1).

Table 3.1 User's perspective template.

Who (User)	What (What job is user looking to finish?)	Why (Why is it important for the user?)
User	Needs to do ...	Because ...

3.5.2 Example (Table 3.2)

Table 3.2   User's perspective example.

Who	What	Why
Lin	share menu with customers	it makes it easier for her to decide what to cook
Lin	know which items customers like the most	so that she could offer to other customers as well
Lin	know which items are not liked by customers	so that she could improve
Lin	get fresh ingredients easily	it is hard for her to drive around during the day
Lin	pack meals	it is easily transportable and she doesn't have to transfer to customer's dishes

3.5.2.1 Guidance

Session Lead

Ask the team to review the journey map and then write insightful points of view for the user.

15-minute Self-brainstorm

Everyone spends 15 minutes to come up with insightful user perspectives.

Team Brainstorm

Everyone shares their user perspectives and lists them in the order of importance for the user. Review all the perspectives and rank them in the order of importance. As you discuss these points of view, feel free to merge the insights and points of view as needed.

3.5.2.2 Document Assumptions

After the session, the session lead should ask the team to write down all the assumptions that you are making and record those assumptions in the assumptions template in Chapter 6.

3.5.2.3 Review Prior Steps

Review the prior steps and adjust as needed with the consensus of the team.

Chapter 4

Stage 2: Devise Solution to Determine Feasibility

This stage is all about generating ideas on HOW to solve the problem that has been identified in the first stage, rapidly prototyping to validate the solution direction and determining the feasibility of the solution in the user's context.

4.1 Step 6: Ideation

Too often we commit the mistake of sticking to the idea that originally came to our minds when we first thought of the problem space. In fact, we don't just think about the problem; most of the ideas are for a specific solution without regard to whether the solution is feasible in the context of the user. What ends up happening is that we polish our idea to a point where it takes the shape of a shiny object ready to be used by the user. However, when the user is first shown the solution, the reality hits us that for reasons unbeknownst to us, the user does not find the solution useful and is not enthused by it. The solution ends up being a shiny ornamental object on the shelf of our metaphoric living space.

To avoid falling into this trap, a methodical and iterative approach needs to be adopted which starts small, gets the user's feedback on all aspects and adapts to the user's needs. The number of iterations could be in the hundreds.

Before you continue the iterations, it is very important to ensure that you are not boxing your solution direction into a narrow direction. It may be helpful to think of your first idea, which you think is game-changing or world-altering or earth-shattering, as a narrow alley in a small town. What you need to do is to step back and stand up on the edge of a hill to have a full view of the landscape of ideas across the entire landscape of ideas. And then you can combine the various ideas into a solution concept that might be worth pursuing. To do just that, have the team do the following before generating ideas:

- Review the design challenge/problem statement. This is about the target the user is looking to hit. (What is the job the user needs to finish? What is the goal the user is looking to accomplish? What is the vision the user is aspiring to realize?) See the value proposition section in stage 3 (5.2) for details.
- Persona
- Current journey
- User's perspectives (Figure 4.1).

Here is an example from a real-life ideation session (Figure 4.2).

4.1.1 Guidance

4.1.1.1 Session Lead

Create a large wall area to collect all ideas and review the following basic brainstorming rules:

1. *Quantity over quality.* During ideation, one must never think of how sophisticated or valuable the ideas are. The goal of ideation is to generate as many ideas as possible. Quantity matters more than the quality of the ideas during brainstorming.
2. *Defer judgment.* As mentioned earlier, we tend to judge not just others but our own ideas. We must not be judging any ideas during brainstorming.
3. *Urge wild ideas.* Another important aspect of brainstorming is that we must not just be content with commonplace ideas which comply with the norms of society, culture or technology. Instead, we must explore ideas which are outside the norms and may even seem somewhat wacky and nonconformist. Discussions with someone of a totally different context than your own would be helpful in bringing forth such ideas. For example, if your team comprises professionals from engineering, sciences or business, talk to people in arts, music, entertainment or

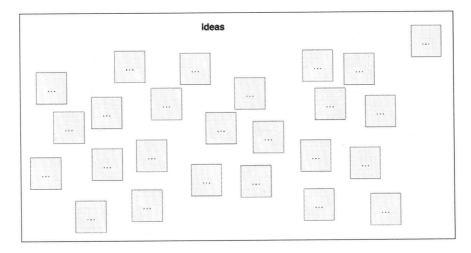

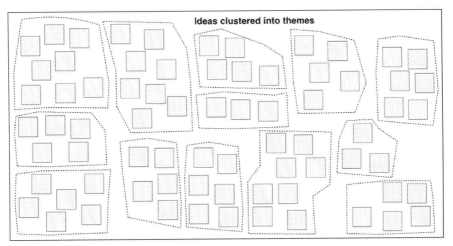

Figure 4.1   Ideas.

sports. You'll be surprised to see how differently these folks think and how unique a perspective they bring to solving your problem.

4. *Focus on the problem.* It's good to think really in different domains, but to ensure you are not distracted, it is important to stick to the problem you are focused on solving.

5. *Build on others' ideas.* Finally, do not just confine yourself to your own ideas. As you review the ideas from other team members, feel free to build on those ideas and connect different ideas together to come up with novel solution concepts. Remember that Apple neither invented the Graphical User Interface nor the mouse, which are so common-place now. They built on the idea of the graphical user interface and the mouse from Xerox.

Figure 4.2   Ideas example.

Once the team is briefed on these rules, start the following self-brain-storming sessions.

5-minute Self-brainstorm:

Each member of the team would already have many ideas to solve the problem for the user. Ask everyone to write all the ideas on sticky notes and place them on the whiteboard.

Ask them to have a quick look at other ideas and then be ready for the next round of ideation.

3-minute Self-brainstorm:

Give the following prompts to instill ideas from the team members. Have at least one round of three-minute self-brainstorming on these prompts.

Prompts around Value proposition.

- How might the user hit the target in a better way?
- How might the user hit the target in a faster way?
- How might the user hit the target in a cheaper way?
- How might the user hit the target in an easier way?

These prompts are likely to generate some usual and commonplace ideas. The following prompts will help you generate out-of-the-box and unusual ideas.

External Prompts.

- Think of your favorite brand; how would that brand solve this problem? For example, how would Apple or Google or Amazon solve this problem?
- Think of another industry; how would that industry leader solve this problem? For example, if your problem is in the consumer products space, prompt the team to think about the hotel industry, the airline industry, the banking industry or another industry.
- Think of your biggest competitor, how would they solve it?

Prompts around Constraints.

Constraints are a great way to push you to think of novel ideas. Using constraints helps in generating unique ideas that no one could have deemed possible before. Introduce some constraints to see how the ideas evolve. Some examples of constraints are as follows:

- What if we only had a quarter of the funds that we currently have – how would we solve the problem?
- What if one of the team members left due to a family emergency – how would we solve the problem?
- What if we didn't have access to X – how would we solve the problem? (X could be any important asset or capability you are relying upon).
- You may also think about the assumptions you have made. Focusing on the critical and major assumptions, consider how you would solve the problem if those assumptions were proven wrong. Review the assumptions section in stage 4 (6.1).

Contrarian Prompts.

Most of the novel business models are a result of teams thinking totally opposite to the conventional wisdom. For example, the conventional wisdom dictates that one should never let strangers come into one's house, let alone spend the night inside. However, AirBNB challenges that exact assumption and built a business exploiting the contrarian approach of generating value from renting a portion of a house to strangers. Another famous example is around hitchhiking. The common cultural narrative is filled with horrific stories, including torture, kidnap and murder when someone hitchhiked with strangers. Parents continue to remind their young and older children to refrain from riding with strangers and avoid taking rides from strangers.

However, Uber and Lyft pioneered the highly successful ride-sharing business model and exploited the completely contrarian view of the conventional wisdom.

■ Push your team to think about all the conventional wisdom related to your problem space that you are operating under. And now imagine you flipped the conventional wisdom upside down; how would you now solve the problem?

Team Brainstorm

Now that you have all the ideas on the whiteboard, have the team review them. You'll see that several themes are emerging in these ideas.

Cluster the ideas according to these themes. You'll be surprised to see the diversity of the ideas and themes. You can consider these themes as a collection of related ideas. Review the ideas individually and in your team. Discuss the merits and demerits of each idea and each theme.

4.1.1.2 Document Assumptions

After the session, the session lead should ask the team to write down all the assumptions made and record those assumptions in assumptions template in Chapter 6.

4.1.1.3 Review Prior Steps

Review the prior steps and adjust as needed with the consensus of the team.

Creativity Requires Time:
Creativity isn't something that you can force in one brainstorming session. One needs to let the ideas percolate into the subconscious in order to have deeper insights as well as "Aha!" moments. It is important that you don't just consider this one session as the final session. This session should be repeated several times. A good rule of thumb is to have the session repeated every week for a couple of weeks. During these subsequent sessions, the quality of ideas improves, and you also have a chance to think about the existing ideas in further depth as well. In addition, do discuss promising ideas with the users whenever you get a chance, so that you can gain further insights and input on the suitability of the ideas in the users' context.

4.2 Step 7: Prioritization

Once you have generated these ideas, it is time to start prioritizing the ideas so that you can filter the ones you could quickly prototype and test with the users. Prioritization could be done in many ways.

- **Dot Voting.** Give 3-5 voting dots to each member and ask them to place them on the top idea clusters/ideas. As teams place their votes, you'll see an emerging theme on the top ideas or idea clusters.
- **2 × 2 Matrix.** One quick way of prioritization is a 2 × 2 matrix with value (to user) on the vertical axis and feasibility on the horizontal axis.
- **Evaluation Criteria.** A more complex and sophisticated way is to identify evaluation criteria, which means identifying some variables which are important for the solution. These may include usability, desirability, technical feasibility, duration, simplicity, business value. Each of the selected variables are assigned weights and the weighted average is calculated to rank ideas.

To have agility in execution, we'll use the 2 × 2 matrix method of prioritization.

4.2.1 Template

Figure 4.3a,b shows how the ideas may look like on the wall as you prioritize using a 2 × 2 matrix.

4.2.2 Example

Figure 4.3c is a snapshot from a real-life session I conducted that showcased idea clusters prioritized on a 2 × 2 matrix.

4.2.3 Guidance

Session Lead

Name each of the idea clusters to easily identify the ideas.

Write the idea-cluster names and selected top ideas on sticky notes.

Take each idea-name sticky note and bring it to the 2 × 2 matrix. Moving the sticky note in a vertical direction, ask the team to evaluate the value of this idea. The ideas which have the most superior value will be placed at the

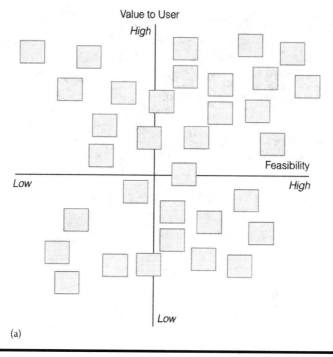

(a)

Figure 4.3 (a) Idea prioritization.

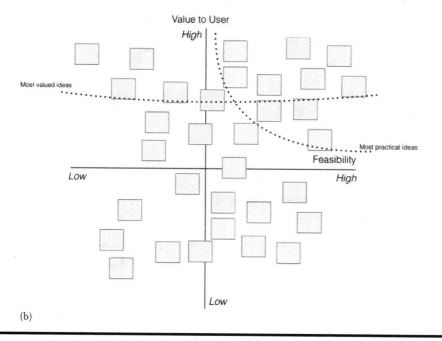

(b)

Figure 4.3 (b) Idea prioritization.

(c)

Figure 4.3 (c) Idea prioritization example.

very top and those ideas which do not have any value will be at the very bottom. All the other ideas will lie somewhere in the middle.

Once the idea has been evaluated on the value axis, staying at the same level, move the idea from left to right on the feasibility scale and ask the team about their view of how feasible the idea is to implement. As you think about feasibility, consider all aspects of feasibility, namely, technical capability, access to expert knowledge, expected duration to implement and any other aspect that influences feasibility.

Based on team consensus, place the idea on the prioritization board.

Repeat the process with all the idea clusters and selected ideas.

Most Valued Ideas

As highlighted in Figure 4.3b, the ideas on the top quarter of the prioritization matrix are the most valued ideas from the perspective of the user based on your understanding. From the user's perspective, realizing these ideas to create a solution would be a tremendous value to the user. However, not all ideas which add value to the users are feasible to implement or viable from a business perspective though.

Most Practical Ideas

The ideas which are both desirable by the user as well as feasible are the ones in the top right corner of the prioritization matrix, as highlighted in Figure 4.3b.

The team should focus on these ideas to move forward.

Note that value to user is based on your understanding, which may or may not be viewed in the same manner by the user. So, it will be important to validate your understanding with the user.

4.2.3.1 Document Assumptions

After the session, the session lead should ask the team to write down all the assumptions that you are making and record those assumptions in assumptions template in Chapter 6.

4.2.3.2 Review Prior Steps

Review the prior steps and adjust as needed with the consensus of the team.

4.3 Step 8: End-to-end Experience Vision

A storyboard is used to convey the future vision of how the user will experience the solution. For each of the boxes below, draw a scene and then write an explanation just below the box, like a comic strip. A best practice in creating a storyboard is to convey the story as follows:

1. Introduce the persona with:
   a. pain points
   b. goals
   c. motivations
2. Convey the user context, including:
   a. triggers in the environment to cause this experience
   b. tools used by the user
3. Show user's experience as they use your new solution.
4. Depict emotions where you see necessary.
5. End with a successful completion of the job.

Show your storyboard to your users/customers and get feedback. Identify opportunities for realizing the solutions using technology in the storyboard.

Don't get hung up on the quality of your drawing. Just using simple stick figures with text in callouts and smileys should be sufficient. The main idea is to show the future journey of the user and get feedback.

For each scene of the experience vision, think about the systems, tools and stakeholders the target user will rely upon. Pay close attention to all the elements that you are expecting the target user to rely upon in the future experience and ask yourself whether this new experience is plausible in the target user's context?

4.3.1 Template (Figure 4.4a)

(a)

Figure 4.4   (a) End-to-end experience vision template.

4.3.2 Example (Figure 4.4b)

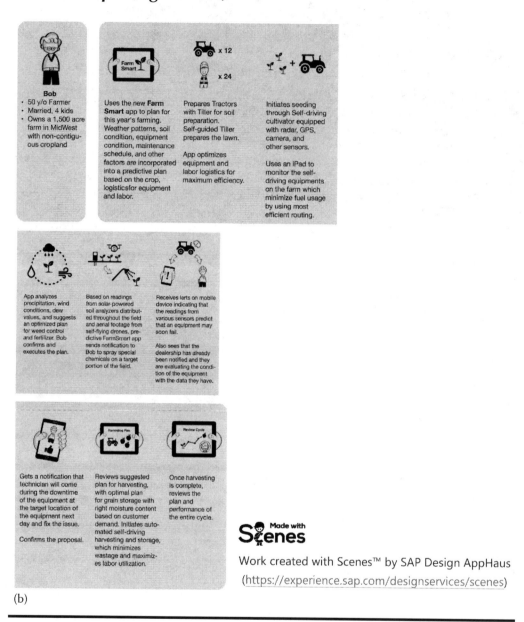

(b)

Figure 4.4 **(b) End-to-end experience vision example.**

4.3.3 Guidance

Session Lead

Collecting the most practical ideas from the prioritization matrix, your goal will be to stitch these ideas together to craft a future experience vision.

Open Collaboration

Once the team understands the various most practical ideas, the team should discuss how these ideas could be brought to bear to create a future that would help solve the user's problem in a manner that would delight the user. You should perform this step with a mind-set which keeps the user as the key protagonist trying to overcome obstacles while performing a job, achieving a goal and realizes the vision. You should be next to a whiteboard with markers to jot down your thoughts and concepts for clarity of understanding and tangibility of concepts. You may leverage the following ways of capturing the essence of the future experience vision:

- Freehand drawing
- Use case modeling
- Flow charting
- Describing in words
- Mind mapping
- Using block diagram

This is a collaborative team exercise. Following the sequence of the storyboard of the future end-to-end experience vision as depicted in Figure 4.3, describe each scene on a sticky note and place on the wall. Continue from the beginning to the various scenes in the middle and conclude with the successful completion of the job.

Don't worry about the quality of the experience vision in the first few iterations. This will require multiple iterations before you are comfortable with the experience vision. As you review and improve the experience vision several times, you'll see remarkable improvements in each iteration. You'll also get an idea whether the experience vision that you are creating makes sense in general and for the user, in particular. Once you and your team are comfortable with the experience vision, use the template and craft the storyboard. Each scene of the storyboard includes an image or diagram depicting the scene as well as a description of the scene in words. Again, do not worry about the quality of the image; just use stick figures and callouts to convey the happenings in the scene.

Once you have the future experience vision storyboard completed, stand back and review it and see if it makes sense. Expect to adjust it as many times as you deem necessary. You may be moving the scenes back and forth, adding or deleting scenes, updating beginning and ending several times before you have a version that you are comfortable with.

Point to Note

Up to this point you have not invested any time and resources in building the actual solution. You have used no technology, no software, no hardware or any other devices. What you have been able to do so far is write down the future vision in the form of a story that conveys the essence of the solution. Doing that also helped you place yourself into your user's shoes to see whether the future experience vision would help solve the user's problem in a manner that is desirable and usable. It is important to highlight that this approach helps you have a view into the future without too much investment. In the next step, we'll explore other forms of prototyping to help you move toward your vision in an agile manner.

4.3.3.1 Document Assumptions

After the session, the session lead should ask the team to write down all the assumptions made and record those assumptions in assumptions template in Chapter 6.

4.3.3.2 Review Prior Steps

Review the prior steps and adjust as needed with the consensus of the team.

4.4 Steps 9 and 10: Prototype and Test

4.4.1 Prototyping

I have already used the word prototype several times in this book. In this step I'll describe in more detail the essence of prototyping, why it is not just important, but critical, and how to go about prototyping your ideas and solutions.

So what is a prototype?

Prototyping is a first preliminary model of a new concept made to test other people's reactions, and to help gain insights into what your idea means to your users. Prototype makes things tangible to improve understanding of the applicability in user's context and identify areas to improve upon. Creating a prototype is a quick way to show how something looks, feels or works. A prototype helps in developing and iterating ideas and can assist you in finding hidden issues with the concept. A prototype also creates a common understanding among stakeholders and aids in redefining the problem.

As the saying goes, "The best way to experience an experience is to experience it..."

In the most simplistic terms, *a prototype is a way to convey a new concept and get feedback in solving a problem.*

There are three aspects to a prototype.

1. A problem that is being solved
2. A concept to solve the problem
3. A way to get feedback

In the previous step, we created an experience-vision storyboard. This was an example of a prototype as well. As you created the storyboard, you highlighted the problem being solved, an approach to solve the problem to get feedback. This will help you have a better understanding of the aspects of the storyboard that makes sense for the user.

A prototype is not confined to specific forms, some of which are mentioned below.

1. *Physical.* If you create a model using cardboard boxes, paper, tape, plastic and other material, it is a physical prototype. You may also use newer mechanisms such as 3D printing to create physical prototypes. For example, to see how a new concept of a reception welcome desk might look and feel in a bank, you may use cardboard boxes to craft the new desk style and place it in the bank to get feedback.
2. *Handwritten on paper.* You may simply use various-sized papers and draw your concepts to create a prototype. In software applications, most often the first version of the prototype is the depiction of the screen using a pen on a piece of paper. These are called wireframes. For creating a prototype of a new mobile app, you may use 3x5-inch

rectangular sticky notes and sketch how the screen might look and how the flow of the screens would be as the user interacts with the mobile app. You may place these sticky notes on a foam board and draw arrows to convey user interactions as well.

3. *Slide show.* You may use a slide-show software such as Microsoft PowerPoint or Apple Keynote and use the native features (such as shapes and lines). Use text and animations to convey your concept and get feedback.

4. *Storyboards.* As we saw in the previous step, storyboards are one of the most powerful ways to prototype. Humans are hard-wired for stories. Stories evoke emotions and leave a lasting impression. All cultures have sustained their traditions over the course of millennia through the use of stories which have transcended generations. That's the main reason why storyboarding an experience-vision concept is one of the most effective ways of prototyping. One of the best storyboarding tools is called Scenes™ by SAP Design AppHaus, which is available at https://experience.sap.com/designservices/scenes.

5. *Role-playing or acting.* Most people don't realize that prototypes do not have to be tangible. Depending on the situation, role-playing or acting could be an effective mechanism for prototyping. One of the most pertinent types of solutions where role-playing has a natural fit is experience design or interaction design. You may also record a video of the role-playing session using a simple smart phone camera to review it later on or show to users to get feedback.

6. *Technical Prototypes.* These days, most of the solutions involve technology, which is primarily software applications either on desktop computers or mobile devices. If your team has the technical skills, you can also create simple versions of software programs to validate your concepts. These software-based prototypes need not have all envisioned functionality or actual data. They can have a simple front-end user interface with non-functional logic. They may only use some dummy data to convey how the concept would work and get feedback. There are many online tools available to help you in prototyping your software concepts. Some of the most popular ones include Sketch, iRise, Axure, InVision and Flinto (Figure 4.5).

4.4.2 Testing

Whatever type of prototyping you adopt, it is extremely important to show the prototype to the user and obtain feedback in a structured manner.

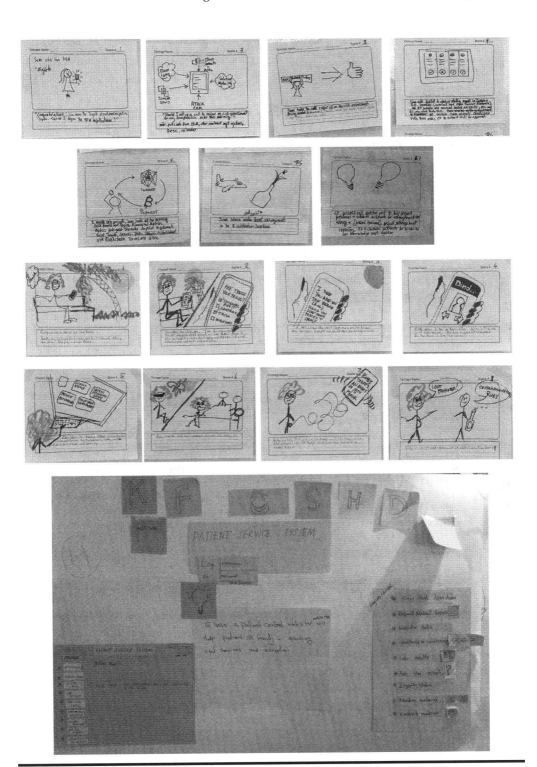

Figure 4.5   Prototype examples.

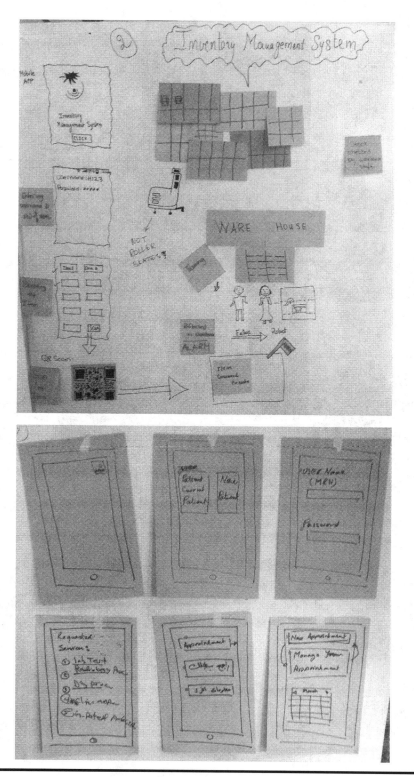

Figure 4.5 (continued)   Prototype examples.

Figure 4.5 (continued)   Prototype examples.

Before we talk about how to gather the user feedback, there are some critical guidelines for obtaining user feedback.

It is best if you could run the user feedback session in pairs. One team member should drive the feedback session as the session lead, and the other should act as a note taker. This is important because you need to have the feedback session run in a smooth manner without the possibility of key insights being forgotten after the session.

4.4.3 Do's and Don'ts for Session Lead

Follow the guidelines for user research highlighted in the user research step in stage 1 (3.2 Research). In addition, here are some do's and don'ts about the user feedback session.

4.4.3.1 Do's

- Do *plan ahead* to meet with the user at a time that is convenient for the user and when the user is least distracted due to work or personal commitments.

- Do inform the user about *the purpose and duration* of the session and highlight why it is important for the user to provide open and honest feedback. The way you position the session has a direct impact on the quality of the feedback. Reiterate that the reason for the session is to devise a solution to solve a particular problem for the user. Mention that this is an initial concept that you want to show to the user and obtain his/her open and candid feedback. Also convey that the input from the user will be used for improving upon the prototype. The duration of the session is dependent on the type and complexity of the solution as well as the available time with the user. Generally, one user feedback session lasts anywhere from 30 minutes to 90 minutes.

- Do *turn all your phones off* and encourage the user to also avoid any potential distractions for the duration of the session.

- Do *make the user at ease* at the beginning of the session and highlight that it is not a test of their abilities but a test to see the *intuitiveness of the user experience*, the *relevance* to the topic and the *functional correctness*.

- Do *explain the scenario* in which the user is likely to be using the prototyped solution. However, do *confirm* whether they agree to the scenario in which they will be using the solution. Do *ask* if there are any other contexts in which the user will be using the solution.

- Do *ask the user to state* their *thoughts, feelings, needs and challenges* during the session.

- Do *keep your words to a bare minimum* during the session. You are interested in getting the user's feedback.

- Do *observe intently* where the user is facing difficulties or is pleased.

- Do *write down* the user's *challenges*.

- Do *write down* the user's *moments of delight*.

- Do *clarify any questions* that the user asks; try to *answer* only in the form of *open-ended* questions.

- Do *note down* all the *questions* the user asks. Questions from the user is an indicator of lack of clarity of the prototype.

- Do act as a *facilitator* only; nothing more.

■ Do *ask for suggestions* for improvement at the end of the session. It is likely that the user will be giving you feedback and suggestions for improvement throughout the session, but it is important to give the user another opportunity to provide any further suggestions to improve the prototyped solution. You may go back to some of the issues highlighted during the session and ask the user for any suggestions for improvement. You have to be mindful of the tone in which you ask for ideas. Your tone must not convey any kind of sarcasm or insult.

■ Do ask if there will be *other users* who could give valuable feedback at the end of the session.

4.4.3.2 Don'ts

■ Don't *help* the user in any way. We have a tendency to be emotionally attached to the amazing experience vision that we have prototyped. However, when the user actually reviews it, he/she inevitably finds some aspects challenging, out of place or totally unusable. At this point, we are naturally inclined to help the user get over the obstacle. This urge must be controlled. The purpose of the session is to intently observe the user as he/she is having these challenges so that you could improve upon the prototype, not to convince the user of its remarkableness.

■ Don't *lead* the user in any way. Similar to the above point, do not lead the user in any way. We are naturally inclined toward helping others. However, this is not the time to help the user, even when the intensity of this urge increases. Observe intently and let the user figure the prototype out.

■ Don't *give any tips.*

■ Don't *give your* preference. Remember that it is not about you or your prototype; it is about the user, his/her problem and getting feedback on the prototype for the solution that you have created. So refrain from sharing any preferences.

■ Don't *judge or belittle the user.* This is a grave sin which a lot of first-timers commit. If you do this, you'll lose any opportunity to gain any valuable feedback from the user in this session or in the future. In fact, doing this will likely help you lose this user forever. It is likely that the user will stumble on several steps while going through the process and using the prototype. Remember, it is not the user's fault or stupidity. It is the prototype that is not meeting the user's needs.

- Don't *give explanations.* When your beloved prototype is being evaluated, you are likely to fall into the mind-set of defensiveness. We have to admit that we don't like it when anyone calls our baby ugly. We fall into the habit of justifying the shortcomings of our prototype. This must be avoided at all costs. In fact, you must continue to thank the user for their valuable feedback.

- Don't *interrupt.* Do not think of this session as a regular conversation, even if the user is an acquaintance. So interrupting the user is never a good idea. However, there is an exception, which is when the user goes away from the task at hand and goes off on a tangent. If that should happen, politely remind the user of the purpose of the session and encourage him/her to continue working with the prototype and giving feedback.

- Don't *laugh* at the user. This is absolutely forbidden. It is in the same category as belittling and insulting the user. Remember that the user is doing you a favor by spending his/her valuable time helping you by reviewing and giving feedback to you on your prototype.

- Don't *ask any questions* during the session. Although some clarification questions are okay, you should refrain from asking questions during the session. If you feel the urge to ask a question, note the topic and ask that question at the end of the session.

- Don't *offer approval or disapproval* with *words, facial expressions or body language.* Remember that you are not judging the user at all. Your main goal is to observe the user and get the feedback on the prototype. Staying neutral is very important throughout the session for gaining effective feedback.

4.4.4 Do's and Don'ts for Note Taker

As a note taker, your primary purpose is to write down all the observations and feedback from the user. These include the user's thoughts, feelings, body language, quotes, needs, challenges, moments of delight, moments of difficulty and ideas. Here are some guidelines for the note taker.

4.4.4.1 Do's

- Do *keep quiet* during the session. You'll feel the urge to speak, suggest or ask questions during the session. Remind yourself of your role during the session and continue writing down the feedback and observations.

- Do *record the session*, with user's permission. You could do a video recording or an audio recording. These recordings can provide valuable feedback later on. If doing a video recording, bring a tripod stand for your video recorder or smart phone.
- Do *observe intently* where the user is facing difficulties.
- Do *write down* user *challenges*. Challenges may include the user getting confused on how to use the solution, the user finding it difficult to use the prototype or the user becoming uninterested.
- Do *write down* the user's *moments of delight*.
- Do *remind the session lead* about his/her role if the lead does not adhere to the guidelines.
- Do *write down* any further feedback, needs or comments that the user shares.
- Do *ask any key questions that were not answered* during the session and were not asked by the session lead toward the end of the session.

4.4.4.2 Don'ts

- Don't *help* the user in any way.
- Don't *lead* the user in any way.
- Don't *give any tips*.
- Don't *give your* preferences.
- Don't *judge or belittle* the user.
- Don't *give explanations*.
- Don't *interrupt* the user.
- Don't *laugh* at the user.
- Don't *ask* any questions during the session.
- Don't *offer approval or disapproval* with *words, facial expressions or body language*.

Diversity of user feedback

It's important to get feedback not from just one but from many users. Having feedback with many users reduces the bias from individual users and helps you see patterns across a wide range of users. This affords you a better chance of meeting the needs of more users.

As you get feedback from several users, it is helpful to alternate roles between session lead and note taker in your team.

4.4.5 User Feedback Template (Figure 4.6a)

During the user feedback session, the note taker should take the Use Feedback Template with him/her to record what the user liked, what the user didn't like or faced challenges with, what are the questions that user asked or that emerged as part of the feedback session and if any new ideas were either shared by the user or emerged during the session.

Please note that you may also take the templates for empathy map with you during these feedback sessions. However, I have noticed that having a complex template is not the most effective way to record feedback. You may update your empathy map as a result of the feedback session later on.

4.4.6 Example

Here is an example from a user feedback session in Figure 4.6b.

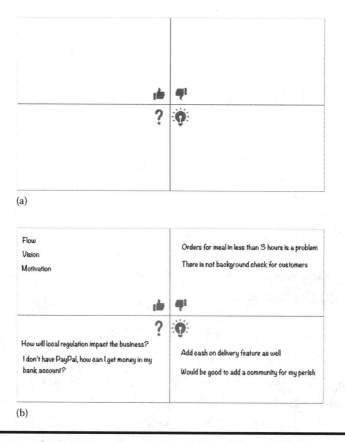

Figure 4.6   (a) User feedback template. (b) User feedback example.

4.4.7 Guidance

Session Lead

Draw this template on a whiteboard and select sticky notes of different colors for each user. This will help you later in tracing specific feedback to specific users.

Select the first user and review the notes of the feedback session. As you go through the notes, write down key points on sticky notes and place them in the appropriate quadrant of the feedback template. It is very important to discuss key insights and not just get hung up on the mechanics of the process. Also, discuss how best to incorporate the feedback into the next iteration of the prototype.

Repeat this for all the other users.

Once you have all the feedback gathered on the template, start reviewing the combined feedback in each quadrant: Like, dislike, questions and ideas. You'll see themes emerging in every quadrant. Cluster those insights and plan on incorporating those insights into the next iteration of the prototype.

4.4.7.1 Document Assumptions

After the session, the session lead should ask the team to write down all the assumptions made and record those assumptions in assumptions template in Chapter 6.

4.4.7.2 Review Prior Steps

Review the prior steps and adjust as needed with the consensus of the team.

4.5 Step 11: Use Case

A use case explains how a user interacts with the solution for a perceived benefit. It is important to understand that the benefit may not be tangible and real – it could be emotional or psychological. Most teams fall into the trap of just focusing on the capabilities or features of the solution and do not put an effort into understanding how that particular capability benefits the user. To be able to do that, you must have empathy with the user. By now you should have spent enough time with the user and have understood his/her thoughts and feelings well enough at a deeper level to be able to understand the kind of benefit the user is likely to derive and perceive.

To be able to understand how your solution capabilities benefit the user, think about whether your solution is able to help the user hit the target *Better* for Quality advantage, Faster for Efficiency advantage, Cheaper for Cost advantage or Easier for Experience advantage.

Hitting the target could be helping the user *Finish a job, Accomplish a goal* and *Realize a vision.*

Review the value proposition section in stage 3 to gain deeper understanding of these concepts (Section 5.2).

4.5.1 Template (Figure 4.7)

Use this template to document use cases that are enabled by your solution for your user.

User	Action (and context)	Result	Hit the Target (Job, Goal or Vision)			
			Better	Faster	Cheaper	Easier

Figure 4.7   User case template.

4.5.2 Example (Figure 4.8)

Here is an example of how the use case template could be filled out.

User	Action (and context)	Result	Hit the Target (Job, Goal or Vision)			
			Better	Faster	Cheaper	Easier
Lin	Can share menu with customers	it makes it easier for her to decide what to cook	x			x
Lin	Knows which items customers like the most	Is able to cook what is needed and avoid food waste	x		x	
Lin	know which items are not liked by customers	so that she could improve recipe		x		
Lin	Can order fresh ingredients	She doesn't have to leave home during day time	x			x
Lin	Sell home cooked meals from home	She can help support her family	x	x		x

Figure 4.8   User case example.

4.5.3 Guidance

Session Lead

Draw the table on the whiteboard, and collaboratively in your team, capture the key capabilities in the form of statements reflecting benefit to the user. Think deeply on the actions the user will take while using your solution and the beneficial result that he/she will derive.

For each of the use cases, mark whether the result is a better, faster, cheaper or easier way of hitting the target – completing a job, achieving a goal or realizing a vision.

4.5.3.1 Document Assumptions

After the session, the session lead should ask the team to write down all the assumptions made and record those assumptions in assumptions template in Chapter 6.

4.5.3.2 Review Prior Steps

Review the prior steps and adjust as needed with the consensus of the team.

4.6 Step 12: Experience Implications

Before you continue to build a productive solution or consider business value aspects, it is important to look at the implications of your future experience vision. These implications could be both dependencies and influences on other entities that may improve or diminish the overall value of the solution.
Implications should be considered from the following three angles:

1. *People.* All connected or influenced stakeholders who are likely to be impacted by the solution.
2. *Process.* If the solution is part of a larger process, then which internal and related processes are likely to be impacted by the solution or will impact the implementation of the solution? This is primarily relevant for solutions that are suited for enterprises. However, it may also be relevant for personal/consumer solutions. For example, if your solution helps consumers with low credit get loans to buy used cars, your solution will be part of a larger car-buying process which includes searching for cars, checking credit worthiness, affordability calculations, car inspections, car valuation, warranty, delivery, service, maintenance cost estimate and so on. Thinking of all these related processes will help you have a better idea of the value proposition and business model of your solution.
3. *Technology.* Finally, your solution is likely going to be leveraging technology. Thinking about various technology elements will help you have a better way to build and position your solution. As you think about the technology, think about the various systems, social and professional networks, data, algorithms and other tools that either you'll be leveraging for your solution or must be thought about for implementation of your solution.

4.6.1 Template (Figure 4.9)

This template is used to identify people, processes and technology implications for building a solution. It highlights obvious and latent needs and considerations early on.

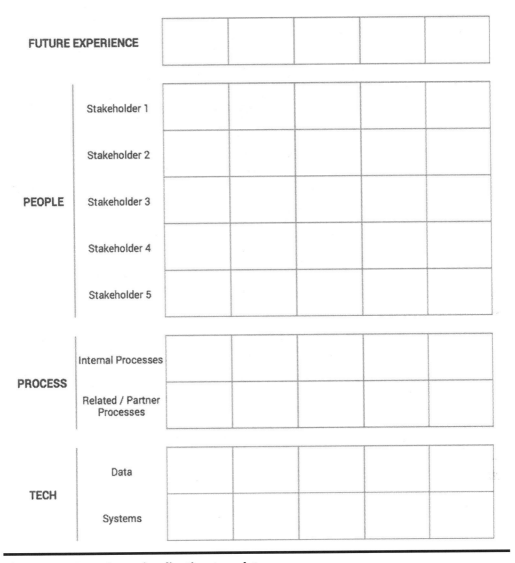

Figure 4.9   Experience implication template.

Based on the future experience that you have envisioned and depicted in the storyboard, think about other dependencies in terms of expectations from other stakeholders. Also consider the impact on internal and external processes and the system and data dependencies.

4.6.2 Example

An example of how experience implication template could be filled is shown in Figure 4.10.

		1	2	3	4	5	6	7
	FUTURE EXPERIENCE							
PEOPLE	Stakeholder 1	Project Manager	Project Manager	Project Manager	Team Members	Finance	Team Members	Team Members
	Stakeholder 2	Client	Client	Client	Project Manager	Project Manager		Project Manager
	Stakeholder 3		Risk Manager	Executive Sponsor				
	Stakeholder 4		Executive Sponsor					
	Stakeholder 5		Controller					
PROCESS	Internal Processes	SOW creation	Solution Marketing		Project Tracking	Invoicing, Payments		Documentation
	Related / Partner Processes		Partner Manager	Partner Manager		Accounts Payable	Partner evaluation	
TECH	Data	Customer and team information	Calendar availabilities	Contract		Invoice, Payment receipt		Project Artifacts
	Systems	Customer Relationship Management	Customer Relationship Management Contract Mgmt system	Contract Mgmt system	Project Management System	Finance System	Travel System	Document Management System

Figure 4.10 Experience Implication Example.

4.6.3 Guidance

Session Lead

Draw the Experience Implications Template on the whiteboard and paste the scenes from the future experience vision on the top row. If you have three team members, assign each member to focus on specific implications – people, process and technology. It will be helpful to have the team members with capabilities in each area to be assigned those areas. For example, the member focused on technology (a Chief Technology Officer in a start-up) should be focused on technology implications.

5-minute Self-brainstorm

Point out the first scene and ask each member to think about implications in their area and write the implications on sticky notes.

Team Brainstorm

Once the self-brainstorming session completes, each team member should paste their sticky notes at the appropriate swim lane/row and explain their ideas. Have immersive discussion to ensure the whole team has a comprehensive understanding of the implications in all dimensions.

Move to the second scene and repeat the process. Continue moving through your experience vision and complete the entire Experience Implications Template.

4.6.3.1 Document Assumptions

After the session, the session lead should ask the team to write down all the assumptions made and record those assumptions in assumptions template in Chapter 6.

4.6.3.2 Review Prior Steps

Review the prior steps and adjust as needed with the consensus of the team.

Chapter 5

Stage 3: Craft Business to Know Viability

Most start-ups fail not because they didn't find the right problem to solve for the user demographic or that their solution lacked technological prowess but because they could not figure out a sustainable business model for their idea. Similarly, most hugely successful start-ups didn't just understand the problem of their user demographic and build solution to solve the problem. They crafted a business model that made them hugely successful. For example, Google, while helping users find more relevant websites using their superior algorithm, figured out an advertising business model that until this day generates 9 out of every 10 dollars of its revenue.

It is critical to understand the business context in which you are playing, the value proposition to your user demographic and various aspects of the business model as you embark on this exciting journey. This stage will guide you through all the key aspects of crafting a business.

5.1 Step 13: Business Context

Before we craft the value proposition for your business model, it is important to understand the external context your business will be operating in. Statistics do not favor the success of start-ups. Only one out of 10 start-ups ends up achieving some form of success. Most start-ups just focus on their idea and do not spend enough time thinking about the externalities affecting their business. These factors represent many aspects, the most important of which include the following:

- *Technology.* The adage "change is the only constant" is perhaps most pertinent now and applies more to technology than any other aspect of society. Not only is the rate at which technology changes exponential but the pace or the frequency of the cycle of change is also following an exponential curve. This change spans all types of technologies, including computing, storage, networking, mobile access, nanotechnology, digital biomedicine, artificial intelligence, pico-technology, internet of things, crypto-currency, autonomous robots and cars. Unless you have a close eye on the technological trends likely to impact your business model, you run the risk of being disrupted. These technological trends, if leveraged properly, also present an opportunity to craft innovative solutions. Understanding the near-term and long-term technology trends will also help you take advantage of emerging technologies to build your business model around.
- *Business Models.* Traditional business models are giving way to new models which are upending centuries-old ways of doing business. Some of the examples include the following:
  - *Online retailing,* which incurred fractionally lower cost for every dollar of revenue it earns compared to traditional brick-and-mortar retail operations.
  - *Peer-to-peer business model,* such as the ones exploited by Uber, Lyft and AirBNB, have upended traditional taxi operations and rental car companies by matching consumers and providers with extra capacity (in their cars or homes) to consumers who need to use that capacity in a user-friendly manner using smart phones.
  - *Digital platforms* such as Amazon Web Services are uprooting traditional IT infrastructure companies and IT departments at enterprises as well as enabling start-ups to prototype and build their companies on scalable and practically unlimited computing, storage and networking capacities. Other examples of digital platforms include search platform like Google and social platforms such as Facebook and Twitter. These platforms are used by hundreds of millions and even billions of people around the world. They have uprooted the traditional advertising business model with their exponentially superior capabilities in micro-targeting and allow businesses to

understand the effectiveness of their marketing campaigns in a manner not possible in the past.

– *Cross-industry* reach has blurred the lines between industries. This trend has allowed competition from players in industries outside the typical boundaries to disrupt historical business models. A prime example includes Apple, which is not just a consumer products company delivering technology-based products but is also a mobile phone provider and an entertainment provider that sells digital entertainment (video, music and games). Apple is now venturing into health care through its wearable devices and also provides cloud-based storage capabilities to consumers. Another example is Amazon, which started as an online bookstore and is now the biggest online general retailer and the fastest-growing retailer. Amazon is also a home-services provider, with grocery delivery and retail outlets (the Whole Foods chain is owned by Amazon) and is the leader in cloud services through Amazon Web Services. Amazon is also venturing into the prescription drug market and aiming to disrupt the health care industry through its joint venture with Berkshire Hathaway and JP Morgan Chase. More and more cellular service providers are looking for ways to leverage their vast infrastructure to provide other services, including banking services and entertainment content distribution.

– *Customer experience* has become a competitive weapon for newcomers. Just over the past 11 years, since the advent of the first iPhone back in 2007, consumers' expectations of consumer experience has altered dramatically. Even though when the iPhone 1 was launched it had less than 50% of the features of the existing smart phones in the market – Blackberry, HTC, and so on – the consumer experience of the iPhone was so much better that consumers flocked to buy it, even though the iPhone was more than three times the cost of the existing smart phones. Since then, companies have realized that they can compete and build their business model around a superior customer experience.

– *As-a-Service* business models have emerged over the last decade as a viable competitive alternative. Consumer behavior is moving away from owning products to consuming the service those products offer. This can also be thought of as a *utility-based* business model. What happened to utilities (electric and gas) decades ago is now happening to other products. Some examples include Software-as-a-Service, Platform-as-a-Service, Infrastructure-as-a-Service, Book-as-a-Service, Car-as-a-Service, Jet Engine-as-a-Service, Fuel-as-a-Service. Every industry is exploring and experimenting with As-a-Service business models.

  – *Digitalization of physical products* is also presenting novel business model ideas. Those products which used to be physical are now becoming digital. Examples include encyclopedias, books, magazines, home keys, medical records, training and education.

  – *Data-driven* business models will dominate the future of every industry. The human race has produced more data in the past two years than was produced cumulatively since the first homo sapiens walked on Earth. With the advent of massive social networking platforms enabling users to share not just text but multimedia content, the rise of internet-enabled devices (often called the Internet-of-Things or IoT) and online systems, the amount of data generated every minute is staggering. It is going to continue growing at an exponential pace, generating massive amounts of data. Start-ups and enterprises are investing massive amounts of capital in gaining insights from this data and enabling data-driven business models where the revenue is generated from selling insights from the data rather than the data itself.

■ *Competition.* You must look at the current and future competitive trends that will be impacting your business model. Remember that competition is not considered just as a direct product substitute. Instead, your competition is anything that replaces the need to use your solution to solve the user's problem. For example, for McDonald's, competition is not just Burger King, Carl's Junior or other fast-food chains; competition for McDonald's is every restaurant, grocery store and home kitchens that serve or help users cook not just the three meals a day but also snacks and drinks.

■ *Industry.* It is also important to consider the emerging trends in the industry you are playing. From the business model discussion earlier, you can appreciate that your industry is likely going to be encroached by players and dynamics outside your industry domain. Having a wider lens to understand industry trends inside and outside your industry will be beneficial to crafting your business model.

■ *Macroeconomic.* Business models aren't crafted in vacuum. Your company, your team, customers, partners and offices are all part of the

macroeconomy. At the smallest level, the neighborhood, the community and city and, on the larger level the county, state, country and
beyond are influenced by numerous trends, including political climate,
environmental changes, economic situation and demographic trends.
In addition, your business model may also be affected by evolving
demographic trends which includes behavioral expectations of various
demographics. Understanding these short-term and long-term macroeconomic trends will help you craft a business model that is more
sustainable.

■ *Others*, including regulatory environment. Beyond the ones just mentioned, there could be several other local or global trends that might
be of relevance to your business model. Thinking about any trend that
might impact any aspect of your business model helps you be better
prepared in warding off unexpected obstacles.

5.1.1 Business Context Template

Use template in Figure 5.1a to explore the business context for your idea.

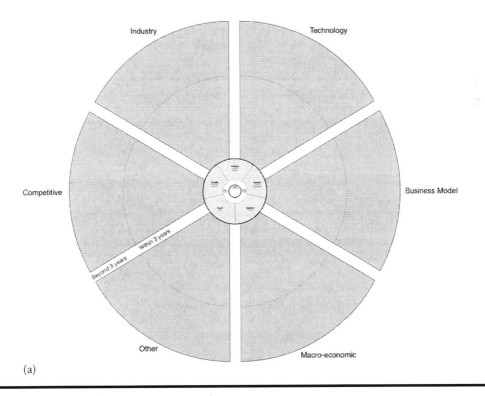

(a)

Figure 5.1 **(a) Business context template.**

5.1.2 Example (Figure 5.1b)

Here is an example of business context for an idea around employee productivity business.

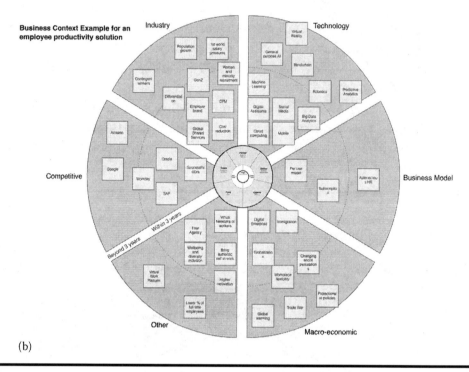

(b)

Figure 5.1 **(b) Business context example.**

5.1.3 Guidance

Session Lead

Draw the template on a whiteboard. Make sure it is drawn large enough so that all the ideas from brainstorming can fit inside it. In general, a circle with five-foot diameter would suffice. Do not worry about drawing the inner smaller circle, which is the business model that will be worked on in the next few steps.

Select the first trend – technology – to work on first.

10-minute Self-brainstorm

Ask each team member to think about all the technology trends relevant to your idea (problem and solution) likely to be considered or that will have an impact in the next three years horizon. Give five minutes to the team.

Now ask each team member to think about all the technology trends relevant to your idea (problem and solution) likely to be considered or that will have an impact beyond the three-year horizon. Give five minutes to the team.

Team Brainstorm

Ask team members to come to the whiteboard one by one and paste their sticky notes in the relevant technology section. Also discuss whether the trend is to be considered for the near-term horizon (less than three years) or longer term horizon (beyond three years). As each team member pastes each sticky note on the wall, ask them to explain how it impacts your idea. Encourage discussion to ensure all ideas are captured and discussed. You can expect to have some difference of opinion around the horizon (within three years or beyond) in which the particular trend would impact the business model.

Complete the Business Context Map

Repeat the self-brainstorming and team brainstorming steps for all the other dimensions of the business context map.

- Business Model
- Competition
- Industry
- Macroeconomic
- Others

5.1.3.1 Document Assumptions

After the session, the session lead should ask the team to write down all the assumptions made and record those assumptions in assumptions template in Chapter 6.

5.1.3.2 Review Prior Steps

Review the prior steps and adjust as needed with the consensus of the team.

5.2 Step 14: Value Proposition

The core of the business model is the value proposition of your solution to the customer. To be able to understand how your solution capabilities benefit the customer, consider an archer who is aspires to hit the target using his bow and arrows. You, as an entrepreneur, want to build a solution that helps the customer hit the target:

- *Better.* If the solution improves the way the particular user went about fulfilling his/her need, the solution value proposition is that it helps the user hit the target better. The benefit could be helping the user maximize some aspect that he/she intends to maximize or alleviate a pain that the user is wishing to minimize. Better translates into a competitive *Quality Advantage* for the customer where the solution is more accurate and consistent in delivery of value.
- *Cheaper.* If the solution lets the user hit the target at a lower cost, the value proposition is cheaper. This translates into a competitive *Cost Advantage* over your competition.
- *Faster.* If the solution lets the user hit the target in a shorter amount of time and permits hitting more targets than it used to hit, your value proposition is faster. This translates into an *Efficiency Advantage* over your competition.
- *Easier.* If the solution helps the user hit the target in an easier way, the value proposition is easier. If the user is able to hit the target with more ease, comfort, pleasure, delight or novelty, it translates into an *Experience Advantage* over your competition.

The target could be helping the user do any of the following:

- *Finish a job.* The famous "Jobs to Be Done" concept from Clayton Christensen of the Harvard Business School describes it well. In short, when a user buys a product or service, he/she actually is hiring that product or service to do a job. For example, you buy a thermometer to do the job of measuring your body temperature. You buy a car to do the job of transporting yourself from one location to another as well as doing the job of projecting a specific image about yourself to your friends, family and strangers.
- *Accomplish a goal.* We are a collection of jobs that we do on a daily, weekly, monthly or yearly basis. Each specific job helps us accomplish a goal. For example, we buy a car to help us do the job of going from our home to work, and by doing this job we are accomplishing the goal of reaching work or back home in a timely fashion.

■ *Realize a vision.* As we think more deeply and abstract the concept to a higher level, the goals that we accomplish in life helps us realize our vision about our life. Continuing the example of owning a car, which helps us achieve our goal of reaching our required destination in a timely and comfortable fashion, we realize our vision to provide for our family, maintain our relationships, earn a respectable living or spend quality time with our family by driving in a comfortable car that can reliably transport us from one location to the next (Figure 5.2).

To help you understand the various aspects of the target, imagine the following analogy of a high school soccer team hoping to win the upcoming state championship. To win the championship, they have to win many games in the tournament. To win a game, they need to score against the opponent and block opponents from scoring. To achieve that, they need to plan, practice and execute on the strategy. In addition to playing the games, they need to have a place to gather, practice, work out and so on. The coach needs a way to build a team, evaluate and select players, measure and record performance metrics and do many other jobs.

In this case, the vision of the team is to win the championship.

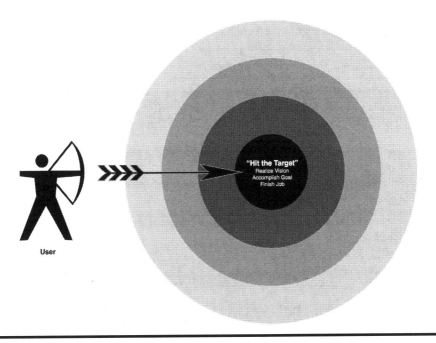

Figure 5.2   Hit the target.

The goal is to win individual games of the tournament against several opponents.

The job that they need to finish is score goals and block goals against them during the game. There are also jobs which need to be performed before the game and afterward, such as practice, plan, execute and review. Jobs could also be considered as actions by the players on the field, such as passing the ball between the players, intercepting the opponent passing and so on (Figure 5.3).

Now imagine a business example. We have all been used to calling ride-share services such as Uber and Lyft for our needs to go from one place to another. These ride-share companies help users solve the problem of going from one location to another. Now consider that these companies are ideating on newer revenue streams. They can consider the segment of working parents who need to have a safe way of taking their children from home to school and activities and back home. In this scenario, they will be helping customers do the job of dropping kids to school, picking them up from school and dropping them at an after-school activity and then picking them up from the after-school activity location and taking them back home. The job still remains picking from a location and dropping to a location, but the goal for the parents is to have a child-safe, reliable and trustworthy way of picking up and dropping off kids. And the vision is to ensure the intellectual and psychological well-being of the kids and their parents' freedom to focus on their daily routine instead of worrying about leaving work earlier to pick up and drop off kids.

As you think about your product or service, have a clear understanding of how you are helping the user in realizing a vision and accomplishing a goal as the user finishes a job using your solution.

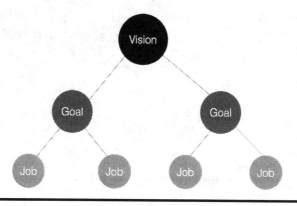

Figure 5.3   Vision, goal and job.

Once you have this clarity, you can achieve differentiation by enabling the user to hit the target in a manner superior to what the current and future alternatives can do. This superiority or competitive advantage could be a solution that is:

- Better – Enabling quality advantage
- Faster – Enabling efficiency advantage
- Cheaper – Enabling cost advantage
- Easier – Enabling experience advantage

5.2.1 Template (Figure 5.4a)

Use template 5.4(a) to document your value proposition.

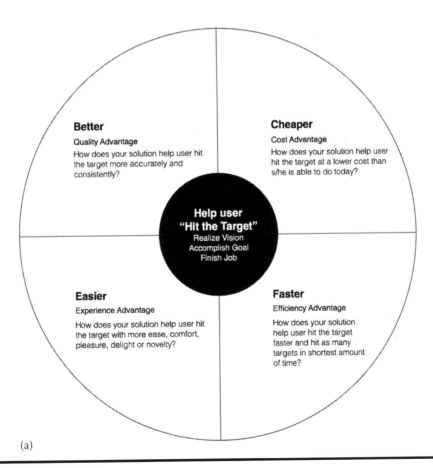

(a)

Figure 5.4   (a) Value proposition map.

5.2.2 Example

Figure 5.4b gives you an example of how your template should look once filled completely.

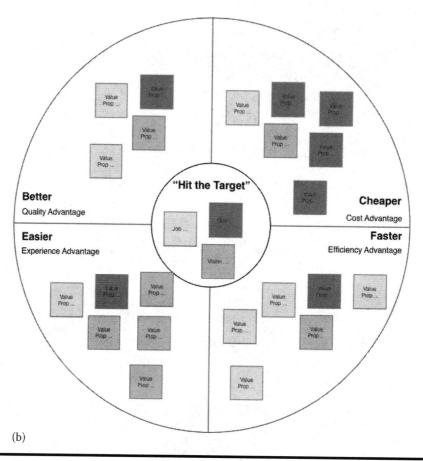

(b)

Figure 5.4   (b) Value proposition map example.

5.2.3 Guidance

Session Lead

Draw a large circle on the whiteboard (about five feet in diameter) and a concentric inner smaller circle (about one foot in diameter), review the use cases created in stage 2 (4.5) and discuss and write down the target your solution will help customers hit in the following manner.

Select three colors of sticky notes. One color will be for jobs, the second color will be for goals and the third color will be to document the customer vision.

Using the appropriate colored sticky notes, write the jobs your solution will help the user to finish, the goals your solution will help the user to achieve and the vision your solution will help the user to realize. Paste these sticky notes in the inner circle.

3-minute Self-brainstorm for Each Job, Goal and Vision

Selecting each job, goal or vision from the inner circle, give the team three minutes to write down how the solution helps the user hit the target better, cheaper, faster or easier. Make sure that you use the same color sticky note as the job, goal or vision. It will be helpful to review the use case step your team would have done earlier as well.

After each round, ask the team members to come and paste the sticky notes on the appropriate quadrant of the value proposition map.

Team Brainstorm

Once all the ideas are up on the wall, review them within the team, discuss the value propositions and clarify understanding. You'll see themes emerging across the four quadrants. Cluster the related sticky notes into themes to clearly see your solution's value proposition for your customers.

5.2.3.1 *Document Assumptions*

After the session, the session lead should ask the team to write down all the assumptions made and record those assumptions in assumptions template in Chapter 6.

5.2.3.2 *Review Prior Steps*

Review the prior steps and adjust as needed with the consensus of the team.

5.3 Step 15: Business Model

As mentioned earlier, the business model is the most crucial and perhaps the most difficult part of designing a business. It involves all aspects of the business, from customers to operations to partners to funding and revenues. There have been numerous frameworks that have gained popularity over the last several decades. These frameworks range in complexity from highly sophisticated analytical models to basic napkin-sized versions for quick-and-dirty analysis. The framework that I'll describe here lies somewhere in the middle and can be used by anyone starting a new venture. It neither requires complex analytical skills nor is too simple to have meaning.

Here we go (Figure 5.5):

A business model is all about one thing – VALUE.

We have so far discussed the value your solution will bring to your customers by solving their key problems in the context in which the problems are most relevant for the customers. That's how we have been able to craft the value proposition for your target customer demographics. Up until now, we have been focused on discovering the problem, prototyping an experience vision that would solve that problem and validating the approach with key customer stakeholders. This has resulted in having a good grasp of the value proposition for the customer.

The value proposition makes the core of the business model. Regardless of whether all the other components work out or not, if the value

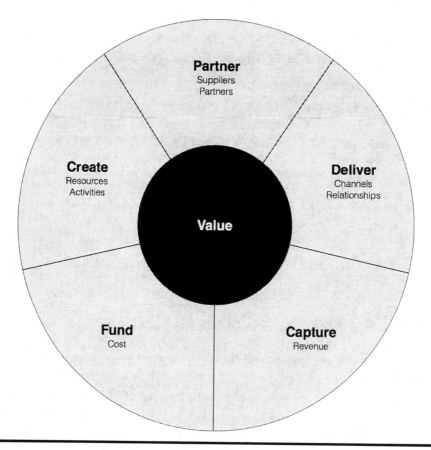

Figure 5.5   Business model framework.

proposition doesn't work out, the whole business model collapses. The value proposition could also be considered as the foundation of any business model.

There are six key components to a business model.

- *Value Proposition.* The first component that we have been discussing so far focuses on understanding what problem is being solved, for whom and why it is worth solving.
- *Value Delivery.* How will the customer know about the product or service being offered, and how will the value be delivered to the customer?
- *Value Creation.* How will you build the product or service and what capabilities are needed to build the solution?
- *Value Partnering.* Who do you need to rely upon throughout the value chain? Who are the external players you need to partner with in this endeavor, and why would they want to partner with you?
- *Value Capture.* How will you generate revenue from customers? Who will pay for your solution? How much will you charge?
- *Value Funding.* From where will you get the funding to support your venture through the early stages and scaling aspects? (Figure 5.6).

Although any sequence could be followed to complete the Business Model Map, a logical sequence would be the following sequence:

- Value Proposition
- Value Delivery
- Value Creation
- Value Partnering
- Value Capture
- Value Funding

5.3.1 Value Proposition

You must have realized by now that from the start of this book until now, the key focus has been to understand the value proposition to the customers – the inner circle of the map. Value proposition essentially answers the question: "WHY is the venture worth doing and whether the problem is worth solving for the key customer segment?" In this section, I'll be giving guidelines on the remaining five components of the Business Model Map.

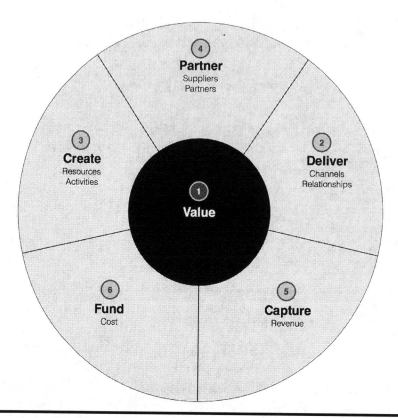

Figure 5.6   Business model framework sequence.

5.3.2 Value Delivery

The quintant of value delivery in the Business Model Map corresponds to accessing customers. Key questions to be answered in this quintant include following:

■ How big is the customer segment where the value proposition is relevant?

■ What is the total addressable market (TAM)? TAM is the portion of the target market that the solution can deliver value to.

■ What is the serviceable addressable market (SAM)? SAM is the portion of the TAM which can be serviced by the business.

■ How will the customers know about your solution and your existence as a business?

■ What channels can be leveraged to access customers? (Online, social platforms, industry forums and events, marketing, face to face, distribution channels, etc.)

- Are there any relationships with customer segments that could be exploited to convey value to customers?
- How can the value be communicated to the customers?
- How much value will the customer perceive of the solution?
- What will be the pricing strategy for the solution?
- Will the solution be readily usable, or will it require implementation services or guidance before it could be used?
- If additional services are needed to make the solution usable, how will those services be provided?
- How will customer support services be provided after sale?

5.3.3 Value Creation

The quintant of value creation is focused on how the solution will be built. At this point, you would have likely iterated on many versions of the prototype to validate the need and solution direction. To be able to build a business, the solution needs to be robust enough for a productive environment so customers could use it in their real context. Key questions to be answered in this quintant include following:

- How will the solution be built?
- What key features and capabilities will be needed for the first release?
- What will be roadmap items for future releases?
- What are the performance objectives for the solution?
- What experience will the solution enable? Rather, how will the solution enhance the customer's experience?

5.3.4 Value Partnering

As a start-up, it is highly unlikely that you'll be able to possess all the necessary resources to create and deliver value to your customers. The quintant of value partnering is all about looking for ways to partner with existing players who could help your business in the value chain and shorten the time to market so you could focus on building your core competency. What you do not want to do is partner on core competency. Ask yourself following questions as you evaluate the need to partner with other entities.

- Can you leverage resources from a partner to build your solution?
- What's in it for the partner to lend you its resources?

- Can you leverage some process expertise from a partner to expedite your solution creation? Examples of this kind of partnership may include manufacturing and quality assurance processes for a partner in Asia.
- What could the partner get in return for expending these processes?
- Can you use technologies from a partner to help you shorten time to market? Examples include Amazon Web Services and Microsoft Azure – these are cloud-based platforms which have become de facto standards for all new start-ups to build their software applications on. Most tech start-ups use APIs (Application Programming Interfaces) from several providers to build their solutions. Some of the most commonly used ones include Google Map API, weather APIs, traffic APIs. In enterprise space, SAP Cloud Platform allows teams to build business solutions as well.
- What would it cost you to use these technology capabilities?
- Can you leverage resources, process or technology from a partner to deliver your product or service to your customer segment? Online retail platforms like Amazon and eBay allow start-ups to make their products and services available to consumers.
- Can the partner help you in gaining visibility in front of the customers who may be their customers as well? Advertising platforms from Google and Facebook are indispensable for reaching the right customer segments for start-ups. In enterprise space, SAP opens access to its 400,000 global customers for start-ups which build solutions on SAP Cloud Platform.
- Can you partner with a player to gain access to a key channel for exposing your solution to customers? For enterprise-focused solutions, there are specialized distributors who help in positioning the solution in front of the right customer groups for a share of the revenue generated through this channel.
- Can you leverage existing relationships between a partner and customers to position your solution? This is most commonly seen in industries where an implementation services provider already has deep relationships with customers and could be leveraged for your solution as well where they could become exclusive implementor of the solution.
- Can you partner with a financial institution to extend credit services for making it easier for value capturing?

Partnerships are all about finding mutual value. As you explore partnerships, think about the value this partnership will bring to the partner.

5.3.5 *Value Capture*

What experience has shown is that value creation and delivery isn't as difficult for start-ups as capturing the value for your business. As you think about capturing value, think about the following aspects.

- Can you quantify the value of the problem you are solving for the customer with your solution?
- Does the customer realize and agree with your estimate of the problem scale?
- Can you quantify the benefit of your solution in solving the identified problem?
- Does the customer realize and agree with your estimate of the solution value?
- Does the customer trust you as a partner?
- What does the customer feel about the problem you are solving? Is there an emotional reason that the customer would be more or less inclined toward solving this problem? For example, if your solution brings efficiency advantage to a client's IT organization that eliminates the need to keep a significant portion of their team on staff, this will create significant emotional distress for the decision maker, not because he/she doesn't want the efficiency gains but because he/she is worried about the well-being of the people who will no longer be needed. In addition, with a smaller team, the CIO's realm of influence in the organization will also shrink – no leader wants to have a smaller team to manage.
- The customer is already continuing his/her business without your solution. How much does it cost currently to operate?
- What are the competitive alternatives a customer has at his/her disposal? How much do the competitive alternatives cost to solve the same problem?
- Does your pricing structure require up-front expenditure for the customer, regular recurring expense (subscription) or a pay-per-use model (utility model)? This makes a huge difference for enterprises, as it translates between a Capital Expenditure (CAPEX) versus Operating Expenditure (OPEX). CAPEX requires additional approvals for enterprises and delays the procurement cycle. For consumers as well, a larger up-front cost acts as a barrier to adoption.

- Many online service providers offer a "Freemium" model which lowers the barrier to adoption by allowing customers to use the service before buying. The Free portion of the model may restrict advance features or may limit the duration of use, which is also called a "trial period." The premium portion of the model is where the value is captured from customers.

5.3.6 Value Funding

Finally, the quintant of funding is as important for a start-up's survival as air is for humans. The graveyard of start-ups is filled with stories where start-ups did an amazing job in identifying a market opportunity, filling a real need and building the initial prototype to solve that problem in a manner that created real value for the customers. They were also able to capture some of the value for their own operations as well, but, as the saying goes, they ran out of runway. Their burn rate (net operating cost per month) became unsustainable, and they weren't able to raise enough funds in time to save the collapse. At the initial stage, the handful of founders could bootstrap and bring the first prototype off the ground, however, to scale, make a production-ready solution and build a lean organization that could serve customers, they needed to raise funds. There are many books that extensively cover the fund-raising aspects of a start-up as well as financial management, but here are some key points to consider:

- Fund-raising means giving a portion of the company to investors. If there is a way to make the start-up self-sustaining, try that first.
- Fund-raising is an exhausting process which takes focus away from operations for a significant period of time.
- Think of a way in which customers could fund the development of the product as well.
- Have a clear understanding of all components of cost and set milestones (aligned with the stages and steps described in this book to have a clear view of the sustainability of the operations).

Resources, Processes and Technology
As you traverse through the Business Model Map, in each of the quintants, discuss and document the resources, processes and technology needed. Here are some of the questions to ask in each of the quintants:

■ What resources are needed? These resources include people and assets.
  – What skills are required?
  – What tools, assets and raw materials are needed?
  – How big of a team is needed to support operations?
■ What processes need to be adopted?
  – What are key activities the team needs to perform on a regular basis?
  – What capabilities are needed?
■ How could technology help in each quintant?
  – Which online services help?
  – What software and hardware will be required?

5.3.7 Template (Figure 5.7)

Use template 5.7 to work on your business model.

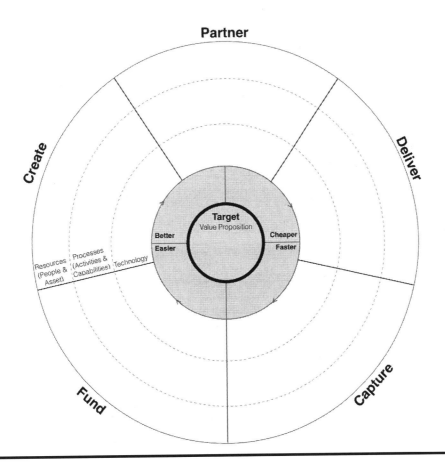

Figure 5.7   Business model framework template.

5.3.8 Guidance

Session Lead

Draw the template on the whiteboard (five feet in diameter) and as a team focus on the Value Delivery quintant. Consider all the questions mentioned about Value delivery earlier and fill in the section. Expect to have lots of questions and interesting discussions.

Have specific discussion around resources, processes and technology that need to be considered for value delivery. Inevitably, discussion would highlight some partnership potentials, which should be documented in the partnership quintant.

Continue the same discussion for Value Creation quintant.

Continue the same discussion for Value Capture quintant.

Continue the same discussion for Value Funding quintant.

Finally, review the Value Partnership quintant.

This exercise will give you insights on all aspects of the business model for your idea.

5.3.8.1 Document Assumptions

After the session, the session lead should ask the team to write down all the assumptions made and record those assumptions in assumptions template in Chapter 6.

5.3.8.2 Review Prior Steps

Review the prior steps and adjust as needed with the consensus of the team.

5.3.9 Bringing It All Together

Figure 5.8 conveys the linkage between all the concepts highlighted to transform an idea into a business. At the core foundation of the business model is the user/customer and the problem you are trying to solve for him/her. In this framework's lexicon, "*Target to hit*" focused on what job you are helping the user to complete, what goal you are helping the user to accomplish and what vision you are helping the user to realize. If you have not understood what the targets are, at not just the rational and analytical level, but at emotional level through building empathy with the user, all

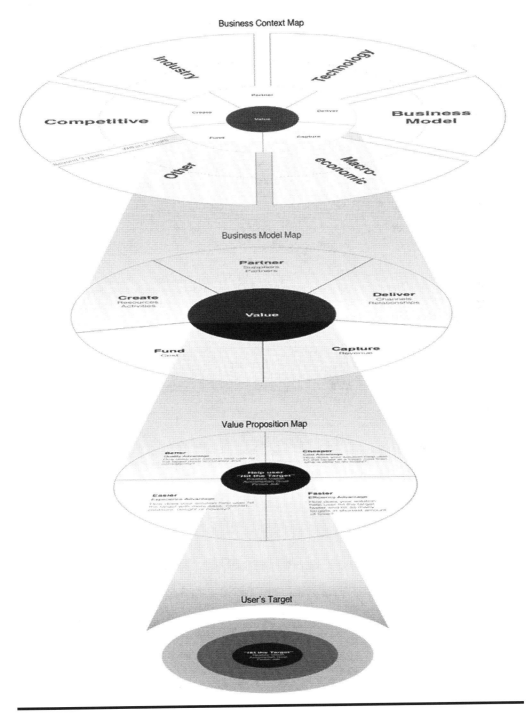

Figure 5.8   Business model framework linkages.

else is immaterial. So spend as much up-front time to uncover those insights as possible. Throughout your iterative prototyping, your goal is to validate that the targets you are helping the customer to hit through your experience vision and solution approach are the ones the customer truly wants to hit.

Understanding the user's problem should be considered the foundation of your business model on which the *value proposition* of your solution is built. Understanding the value that a user sees in your solution approach is extremely important. Whether your solution will help the user hit the target in a *better* way, a *cheaper* way, a *faster* way or an *easier* way will dictate your competitive advantage and thereby your core competency. As you go through this stage, you'll realize the type of advantage your approach has over existing ways of hitting the target, be it *quality, cost, efficiency, experience* or a combination of two or more of these advantages.

With a clear understanding of the value proposition comes the crucial stage of crafting the *business model,* where all aspects of the value chain – *creation, delivery, partnering, capture* and *funding* come into play. Most often, it is neither the problem space that helps you build a sustainable business, nor is it the solution quality, it comes down to a business model. A business model, which is validated by the customers, proven through their wallets, will determine whether your idea can be transformed into a sustainable business or not.

Finally, your business model is not operating in a vacuum. It is heavily and continuously being impacted by the business context you are operating in. Current and future trends – industry, technology, competitive, business model, macroeconomic and others – will shape your business model. Consider these aspects as you build your venture.

One more word of advice before you head to the final stage. As you iterate through all of the steps in this book, your understanding of all the key stages would improve – understanding the problem, devising a solution and crafting a business. If you approach the space with an open mind, you'll see that your idea has transformed into a business which is likely to be drastically different than what was originally conceived. This is very normal and actually a sign that you are finding your way through the entrepreneurial jungle. You'll be doing many pivots before finding the right direction for your business. Be open, fail often and fail early. This framework will help you do just that.

5.4 Step 16: Elevator Pitch

After going through the previous 15 steps, it is important to communicate the value and positioning of your business to the outside world in a manner that is easily understandable and impactful. This step is about helping you craft a succinct message. This messaging could be geared toward potential investors, partners or customers.

An elevator pitch is a common metaphor that has gained wide acceptance. An elevator pitch is a short statement that explains (to investors or other interested parties) the most important facts about your company – all within the time frame of an elevator ride.

5.4.1 Template

5.4.1.1 Short Version

Here is a short version for the elevator pitch:

For	Customer/customer segment,
Our business provides	Solution description
To	Customer Need As Insight (on why it is important for customer),
	Customer Need As Insight (on why it is important for customer), and
	Customer Need As Insight (on why it is important for customer);
Currently,	Competitive alternatives
Lack/are	Competitive advantage(s)
Without this solution, customers will	Impact (loss) of inaction/compelling event for customers to get this solution from you

Here is an example of an elevator pitch of a fictional company called "HomeMeals":

For	Busy professionals and stay-at-home moms,
HomeMeals provides	A mobile social platform
To	Help stay-at-home moms of various ethnic and cultural backgrounds to sell home-cooked meals from their home, As they have the best recipes for ethnic meals which they love to share with others,
	Stay-at-home moms need to earn extra income, As they want to feel an important member of the family and contribute to the community, and
	Busy professionals have access to healthy, home-cooked meals, As busy professionals are always looking for ways to eat healthy, home-cooked meals daily but don't have access to them today
Currently,	Stay-at-home moms use social media platforms to advertise their offerings
Which lacks	Tailored experience for this purpose and limited reach
And	the only option for busy professionals is to cook in the morning or bring food from previous night's dinner to work
Which	They don't have time and discipline for doing
Without HomeMeals	Stay-at-home moms will continue to feel neglected and busy professionals will continue to eat unhealthy expensive meals at restaurants.

This way, you will be able to communicate your message in a compelling manner to pique the interest of the investor, who will likely follow up with more questions or ask you for a follow-up meeting to discuss your offering in detail.

5.4.1.2 Longer Version

Here is a longer and more comprehensive version:

For	Customer/customer segment,
We provide	Solution
To	Customer Need As Insight (on why it is important for customer),
	Customer Need As Insight (on why it is important for customer),
And	Customer Need As Insight (on why it is important for customer);
Currently,	Competitive alternatives, including status quo (how is the problem solved today)
Lacks/are	Competitive advantage
Without this solution, customers will	Impact (loss) of inaction/compelling reason for customer to use your solution
The global addressable market is	X Billion dollars/Y million users
We will focus on	Initial target segment
And reach the customer through	Channel (how would you go to market/how would the customer know about your solution?).
And expect to grow	Growth rate in the first three years or number of users (or growth metric)
Our business model is based on	How will you make money/how much would you charge on what metric?
Our unique selling proposition includes	(Key features, intellectual property, channel relations, access to market,…)
We have a strong team that	Why is your team best positioned to win here?
Finally, our beta/prototype has been available for	Duration since the prototype has been available
And used by	Number of users already trying the beta version
We have already made	X dollars in this initial period
We are looking for	Y dollars
For	Z percent equity stake
To	Explain what you will use the investment for
Ideally, our investor will	Mention if there is any special quality you are looking for in an investor (connections, experience, guidance, industry access, etc.)

5.4.2 Example

Continuing the example of "HomeMeals," here is a longer more comprehensive version of the pitch.

For	Busy professionals and stay-at-home moms,
HomeMeals provides	A mobile social platform
To	Help stay-at-home moms of various ethnic and cultural backgrounds to sell home-cooked meals from their home, As they have the best recipes for ethnic meals which they love to share with others,
	Stay-at-home moms need to earn extra income, As they want to feel an important member of the family and contribute to the community, and
	Busy professionals have access to healthy, home-cooked meals, As busy professionals are always looking for ways to eat healthy, home-cooked meals daily but don't have access to them today
Currently,	Stay-at-home moms use social media platforms to advertise their offerings
Which lacks	Tailored experience for this purpose and limited reach, and
And	The only option for busy professionals is to cook in the morning or bring food from previous night's dinner to work
Which	They don't have time and discipline for doing
Without HomeMeals	Stay-at-home moms will continue to feel neglected and busy professional will continue to eat unhealthy expensive meals at restaurants.

The total addressable market in USA is	$12 billion and reach potential of about 30 million stay-at-home moms and 50 million working professionals.
We will focus on	San Francisco Bay Area and Los Angeles first
And reach the customer through	Social media advertising and ethnic grocery stores
And expect to grow	To a million users within three years
Our business model is based on	Per transaction cut through our platform, similar to Uber, Lyft and AirBNB

Our unique selling proposition includes	Understanding of the ethnic food market and first mover advantage
We have a strong team that	Includes a home chef, a superstar online platform development expert and social media advertising expert
Finally, our beta/prototype has been available for	More than six months in the South Bay region of the San Francisco Bay Area
And used by	More than 500 professionals and 75 stay-at-home moms
We have already made	$50,000 by serving about 15,000 home-cooked meals and are growing at a rate of 20% every month
We are looking for	$1 million
For	15% stake in our business
To	Expand to the entire Bay Area and Los Angeles, stabilize the platform and invest in marketing in these metropolitan areas
Ideally, our investor will	Be passionate about social platforms and peer-to-peer sharing economy, and of course, love home-cooked ethnic meals

As you can see, this version is much more comprehensive and conveys the entire story and future vision in a succinct and compelling manner.

5.4.3 Guidance

Session Lead

This is a collaborative exercise to be done on a whiteboard, in a word-processing document or on a spreadsheet. As you can see, there are a lot of numbers that you have to prepare for this pitch, so you need to do an analytical analysis. There are numerous books and online material which will help you in building the analytical models for your business.

I cannot stress the importance of bringing emotional appeal enough. Although the analytical portion of the pitch is important, the emotional portion supersedes it hands-down. Even if you have all the numbers to back your business plan, if you lack the emotional punch, you won't win the investor.

So practice it and bring the emotional reasons out in your making the pitch to your team. Make sure all team members get a feel for how the pitch will be received by the investors. Once the pitch is well practiced and rehearsed inside your team, have practice pitch runs in front of friends and other mentors or investors who are not interested in investing in this space but would be happy to provide feedback.

During stages 1 and 2, you must have obtained numerous stories from the users. Weave those user stories into your pitch.

5.4.3.1 Document Assumptions

After the session, the session lead should ask the team to write down all the assumptions made and record those assumptions in assumptions template in Chapter 6.

5.4.3.2 Review Prior Steps

Review the prior steps and adjust as needed with the consensus of the team.

Chapter 6

Stage 4: Manage Risk to Handle Uncertainty

The only thing certain in a start-up is uncertainty.

This final stage is all about having an honest discussion and a clear view of all the risks involved in the venture and having a way to prioritize which risks are worth mitigating.

6.1 Step 17: Assumptions

As you have seen throughout this book, at every step in each stage, I have asked you to review this section and document all the assumptions you are making. Risks are the main outcome of assumptions which are not recognized or mitigated. It is important to have an honest discussion about the assumptions you are making for your business through the three stages – understanding the problem, devising the solution and crafting the business. These assumptions should be called out as early as possible and documented in the template mentioned here. It is a live document that should be continuously monitored and discussed regularly.

As you fill out these assumptions, mention the area of the business case it pertains to and the potential impact if that assumption was proven false. And finally, document the steps you should be taking to validate those assumptions.

Areas of assumptions include all aspects of the business model:

- Customer motivations, needs and future behavior expectations
- Value Proposition
- Value Delivery
- Value Creation
- Value Partnership
- Value capturing, including pricing and licensing model
- Value funding, including cost projections
- Experience Implications.
- Resources, Process and Technology dependencies

If during validation you find out that the assumption did not hold ground, then it is necessary to have a critical discussion among the stakeholders to figure out the next steps. It is important to know that at times it is okay if your assumptions do not hold ground. But when that happens, you need to move forward nonetheless. However, this should be a rare event, and the team should agree that they are ready to overcome this obstacle.

6.1.1 Impact

If an assumption is proven false through research, negative consequences on the business would result.

- Impact is *Minor* if the consequence is minimal.
- Impact is *Major* if the consequence is drastic but recoverable.
- Impact is *Critical* if the consequence is catastrophic (Figure 6.1).

These assumptions should be looked at from the lens of an hour glass, where the top half will be filled with these minor, major and critical assumptions at the beginning of the venture. However, as your team goes through the first three stages, these assumptions will be validated, and the bottom half will continue to fill up (Figure 6.2).

You have to note that as you move forward in your venture, the top half will continually be filled with newer assumptions, so do not consider that your initial set of assumptions are all the assumptions you need to worry about.

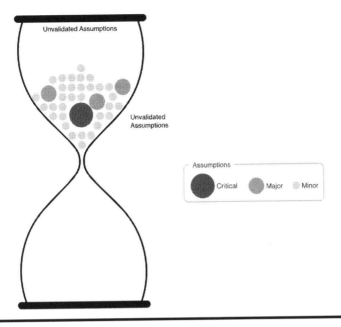

Figure 6.1   Assumptions at the start of the venture.

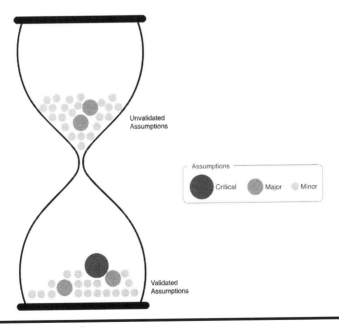

Figure 6.2   Assumption validation during the course of the venture.

6.1.2 Template (Figure 6.3)

Its best to create this assumptions map as a shared spreadsheet, such as Google Sheets, which is constantly updated and monitored regularly.

Status

Set the statuses as follows:

- When a new assumption is created, the status will be *New*.
- Members can change the status to *In Progress* when they are working on an assumption.
- When the assumption is proven true, they would change the status to *Validated*.
- When the assumption is proven false, they would change the status to *Disproved*.

Assumption	Impact	Assignee	Due	Step	Comments	Status

Figure 6.3   Assumptions template.

6.2 Step 18: Risk Assessment

Every venture has inherent risk. And it is a losing battle to try to eliminate the risk altogether. The best that could be done is to have a clear understanding of the risks, their severity or impact on the business and find out ways to mitigate those risks.

So the question is how to have a clear understanding of the risk.

Risk in any business is driven from the assumptions that have been implicitly or explicitly built into various aspects of the business. These assumptions, if proven wrong, have adverse consequences on the business. Having an open and honest assessment of these assumptions will help you to have a clear idea of the risks associated with your business. As we have seen throughout the earlier steps, you have been asked to document all those risks and identify their impact on the business. Now you'll see a simple approach to converting those assumptions into a quantified risk.

6.2.1 Calculation

Aggregate the number of assumptions which have minor impact on the business. You'll have the accumulated value or "Minor Risk Impact Value."

Aggregate the number of assumptions which have major impact on the business and multiply that number by 5. You'll have the accumulated value of "Major Risk Impact Value."

Aggregate the number of assumptions which have critical impact on the business and multiply that number by 25. You'll have the accumulated value of "Critical Risk Impact Value."

Now add the three Impact Values together to find the Risk Score.

$$\text{Risk Score} = \text{Minor Risk Impact Value} + \text{Major Risk Impact Value}$$

$$+ \text{Critical Risk Impact Value}$$

The maximum Risk Score should be 100. At the beginning of the business, the Risk Score is expected to be greater than 100, as there are many assumptions in each stage of the business. The whole idea is that the team should be aware of all the assumptions, and therefore the risks, so that additional effort could be made to mitigate those risks as the idea moves forward. This Risk Score can be shown on a Risk scale as follows so that the team has a clear idea of what needs to be done (Figure 6.4).

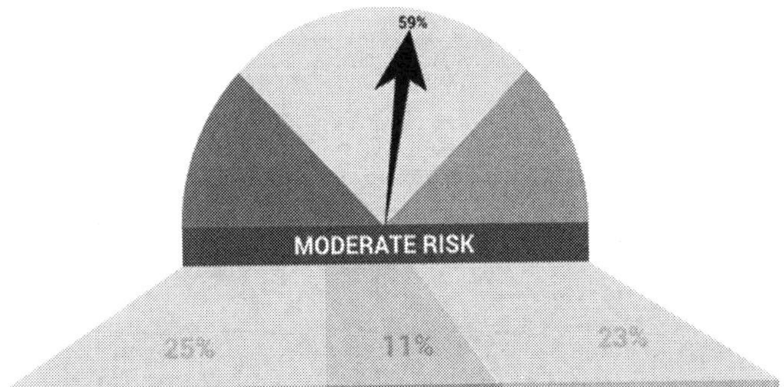

Unvalidated Assumptions	PROBLEM	SOLUTION	BUSINESS
Critical	1		
Major		1	3
Minor		6	8

Figure 6.4   Risk assessment.

You may also break down the risks for each stage to have a clear idea of the risk category. It is imperative to focus on mitigating the critical assumptions first, as those have the most adverse impact on the business. This should be followed by addressing Major risks, which should be followed by taking care of Minor risks.

Chapter 7

Go Ahead and Transform Your Idea

A journey of a thousand miles begins with one step.

I hope this framework will help you transform your idea into a business.

About the Author

Mashhood Alam is a senior innovation leader who has been driving innovation with Silicon Valley's top companies and start-ups for over two decades. Mashhood leverages his technology background, deep business expertise and design-thinking skills to use technology to solve complex problems and make life easier for people.

Mashhood has built products as a software developer, helped launch solutions to market as a product manager, driven strategy for half-billion-dollar product line, spearheaded innovation-led sales programs, driven co-innovation projects with customers in various industries, led digital transformation initiatives for world's top enterprises, advised numerous start-ups and converted several ideas into businesses during the course of his career.

Mashhood has been granted six US patents and won two prestigious design awards, including the Red Dot Award for innovative design concept for a citizen-centric information portal. Mashhood has been a guest speaker at several industry events as well as mentored numerous start-ups in many Silicon Valley boot camps. He regularly speaks to C-level audiences on innovation and digital transformation. He has also been a guest lecturer at various business and entrepreneurial schools, including University of California, Berkeley.

Mashhood holds a bachelor's degree in computer systems engineering from NED University of Engineering and Technology, a master's in systems sciences from Louisiana State University and a master's in business administration from Santa Clara University. He can be contacted at http://www.MashhoodAlam.com.

Index

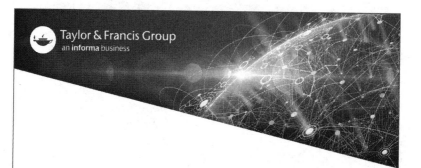